YO-BCT-269

Nowhere to Hide

The Great Financial Crisis and Challenges for Asia

Michael Lim Mah-Hui and **Lim Chin**

INSTITUTE OF SOUTHEAST ASIAN STUDIES
Singapore

First published in Singapore in 2010 by ISEAS Publishing
Institute of Southeast Asian Studies
30 Heng Mui Keng Terrace
Pasir Panjang
Singapore 119614

E-mail: publish@iseas.edu.sg
Website: http://bookshop.iseas.edu.sg

The responsibility for facts and opinions in this publication rests exclusively with the authors and their interpretations do not necessarily reflect the views or the policy of the publisher or its supporters.

ISEAS Library Cataloguing-in-Publication Data

Lim, Mah Hui.
  Nowhere to hide : the Great Financial Crisis and challenges for Asia / by Michael Lim Mah-Hui and Lim Chin.
  1.   Global Financial Crisis, 2008–2009
  2.   Financial crises—Government policy—Asia.
  3.   Asia—Economic conditions—21st century.
  I.   Lim, Chin, 1947–
  II. Title.
HB3717 2008L73   2010

ISBN 978-981-4279-73-4 (soft cover)
ISBN 978-981-4279-74-1 (E-Book PDF)

Cover artwork: Fadzli Amir

Typeset by International Typesetters Pte Ltd
Printed in Singapore by Markono Print Media Pte Ltd

Nowhere
^{to} Hide

Best Wishes,
Mah-Hui Lim

The **Institute of Southeast Asian Studies (ISEAS)** was established as an autonomous organization in 1968. It is a regional centre dedicated to the study of socio-political, security and economic trends and developments in Southeast Asia and its wider geostrategic and economic environment.

The Institute's research programmes are the Regional Economic Studies (RES, including ASEAN and APEC), Regional Strategic and Political Studies (RSPS), and Regional Social and Cultural Studies (RSCS).

ISEAS Publications, an established academic press, has issued more than 2,000 books and journals. It is the largest scholarly publisher of research about Southeast Asia from within the region. ISEAS Publications works with many other academic and trade publishers and distributors to disseminate important research and analyses from and about Southeast Asia to the rest of the world.

Contents

Foreword

Dr Michael Lim Mah-Hui and Dr Lim Chin sent me their latest book on the great financial crisis for comments. I was curious to know what this manuscript would add to the mass of literature and debate that is circulating at this juncture. After reading the manuscript, I am fully convinced that it is a valuable addition to the literature on the subject for several reasons.

First, the book is very lucid, easy to read and simple to understand. Second, it captures history, current context and the way forward. Third, it succinctly presents theory and focuses on policies and institutions rather than abstract thinking or anecdotes. Fourth, it gives an emerging market perspective while presenting in detail the debates on the subject in the western world, in particular the Anglo-Saxon world. Fifth, the book emphasizes the Asian point of view and it is presented in a way that captures the dynamic and evolving interrelationship between Asia and global economy. Finally, the analysis has several original elements in explaining theory and practice in public policies as well as the behaviour of financial markets.

The book analyses the causes or the origins of this crisis at three inter-related levels broadly covering economic and financial theory, financial sector practices, and macroeconomic imbalances and the international monetary system. The authors refer to the belief in Efficient Market

Hypothesis that governed public policies in general and central bankers and regulators in particular as the primary cause of the crisis. I can fully endorse the prevalence of this view even in the year 2006 and early 2007. By then the underpricing of the risks in the financial markets and the dangerous level of macroeconomic imbalances had come to the fore. However, in the interactions between central bankers and market participants exploring methods by which soft landing could be engineered, market participants asserted the view that, interfering with market-determined pricing of risks would be a serious policy mistake.

It is "these same people", as the authors describe, that pleaded and perhaps even demanded massive intervention of public policies within few months of their assertion to the contrary, once the crisis struck. The asymmetrical response of financial markets to the desirable level of public policy intervention seemed to be governed by the benefits that accrue to participants in the financial sector. It is instructive to note that financial markets that were keen on transparency for actions by monetary authorities and regulators have joined hands with authorities to not disclose the terms and conditions of many bailout operations. There is yet another asymmetry in the analysis of market behaviour as well as on the causes and cures for the crisis in advanced economies versus that in emerging market economies. The Asian financial crisis was blamed on crony capitalism and improper corporate governance. But these same practices that are also present in the present crisis are conspicuously absent in Western commentators' analysis.

The Efficient Market Hypothesis has its companion in the modern theory of risks management. However this model did not go far back enough to take into account historical facts and data that impact the present situation. It also does not recognize that financial markets may be dominated more by speculative sentiments and expectation of future changes in price than price based on the need to satisfy wants. Such sentiments often result in herd-mentality. The rapid growth of the financial sector was governed by the belief in Efficient Market Hypothesis, reinforced by technological developments and globalization of finance. Consequently, the financial sector has grown much more rapidly than the real sector leading to dominance by the former. This disproportionate growth between the real sector and the financial sector is an additional set of asymmetry that was analysed by the authors.

At a more general level, it can be argued that excessive state intervention and frustration with stagflation prior to Reagan-Thatcher era, together with intellectual inspiration from the Chicago School, led to a belief that if one gets prices right, all other matters will fall in place. The current crisis has shown that prices may not necessarily be right if public policies are not right. The debates in the post-crisis period indicate that there is still inadequate attention paid to find the right balance between market forces and state intervention. There is still an inclination to treat state intervention as exceptions but painful necessities, and that markets are right except in times of crises. It is also likely that the shape of financial reforms under consideration in the present crisis is influenced by the continued power of the financial industry over policy-makers and politicians.

On par with the faith in Efficient Market Hypothesis is the belief that financial innovations have positive contributions to the economy and society. Even after the crisis, the putative benefits of financial innovations are often reiterated without much evidence. In fact, Paul Volcker, a former governor of the Fed recently stated, "I wish someone would give me one shred of neutral evidence that financial innovation has led to economic growth — one shred of evidence."

This book provides an excellent overview of recent financial innovations. It is clear from the narration that the downside risks are real while the benefits are mere assertions. [There is no empirical evidence to support the view that these innovations have added to efficiency in resource allocation or resource use.) There is some evidence that most of the innovations have resulted in the redistribution of wealth and income rather than an increase in output or employment. There is a reference in the book to the financial innovations that Minsky wrote about in the early 1980s, and how they have become safe by today's standards. Financial innovations that he did not anticipate have now come into existence. The interesting issue is whether the recent innovations that are proven to be unsafe, will also turn out to be safer after regulatory reforms are undertaken. In my opinion there is qualitative difference in the earlier financial innovations and the recent ones. [The earlier innovations improved the efficiency of financial intermediation and contributed to growth of the real sector. The recent financial innovations were mainly meant to side-step financial regulations, in particular capital requirements.] Hence, going forward empirical work on the efficacy of each financial innovation in the context of different countries is warranted.

Chapter 3 is valuable in terms of the wealth of evidence provided. However the evidence is mostly from the United States and it is possible that a similar regulatory capture process is happening in other countries though to a lesser extent. A more fundamental question therefore relates to the reasons for such a comprehensive regulatory capture in the U.S. Financial markets have short-time horizon and political leaders also have similar short-term outlook. They reinforce each other in capturing the regulators. The mainstream academia has also been dominated by those who were willing to contribute to and benefitted from the prevailing ideology and dominance of the financial sector. The revolving door for academics between government, regulatory agencies and financial markets reinforced these linkages and shared interests. The media catered to the demands of consumers and investors and hence the coverage on macroeconomic issues was often underplayed, since it was not of immediate interest to readers.

There is a brief reference in the book to the dominance of "Economic Value Added School of Thought". According to this approach, the objective of the company is to maximize shareholders' value while treating other stakeholders as not very relevant. It is true that this approach resulted in emphasis on short-term and fee-based income with a bias towards excessive multiplication of transactions. It also resulted in mechanisms to circumvent the requirements of regulatory capital. More important the evidence shows that operations in the financial sector resulted in huge remuneration to the management and only a smaller part was available for shareholders. This reinforces the view that linkages formed between senior managers in the financial sector, the government and regulatory agencies enabled regulatory capture.

The treatment of the three macroeconomic imbalances in the book as the fundamental reasons for the global financial crisis is excellent. One observation on the subject of imbalances is of significance: "Just as an organic or biological system becomes dysfunctional where its components are out of balance, the same happens to economic and financial systems when things are not balanced." Considerable attention has rightly been given to explain the issue of global current accounts imbalances in terms of excessive savings in Asia, on the one hand, and excess consumption in America, on the other. Personally and from a technical viewpoint, I take a neutral position as there can never be a world where all countries enjoy current account balance, i.e., are without deficit or surplus. The world economy is a closed economy and surplus and deficit in current accounts have to balance at the global level. The real issue is whether these imbalances are sustainable in an imperfectly globalized world where goods and other factors are freely traded.

Growth and development are ultimately guided by human values such as happiness, well-being, equity and justice. If these values are taken into account to explain the two excesses, then excess consumption by an already rich population is difficult to justify not only from a point of justice but even from a point of survival of the world. Since consumption draws on depletable natural resources, the burden on the global ecological system is aggravated by excess consumption. Using a value-informed approach will

be helpful in determining priorities for correcting global
imbalances and sustainable development. As Mahatma
Gandhi once remarked, there is enough on this earth to
satisfy everyone's need but not everyone's greed. Or put
in another way, the measure of a civilization is not the
amount of desires it can satisfy, but the amount of desires
it can control.

Chapter 5 provides interesting insights into the impact
of the present crisis on Asia, their policy responses and
challenges for the future. It would be useful to supplement
the analysis with more discussion on economic integration
between Japan, China, Southeast Asia and South Asia,
in particular India. India has current account deficit and
is likely to generate such deficits in view of the need
for growth and eradication of poverty. The country has
serious concerns on the volatility of capital flows. There
is recognition of the increasing importance of Asia in
the evolving global economy. Policy-makers in Asia are
assessing the manner in which a new paradigm, in the
post-crisis global economy, could work out for Asia. I
will offer a few thoughts on this subject.

First, there will be massive economic activity in
Asia. Millions will be added to the workforce each year,
and living standards will keep improving. A growing new
middle class will generate huge demand. Urbanization will
lead to infrastructure demand spurring vibrant economic
activity. Asian multinationals could take center stage in
the world in the next few decades.

Second, with an annual addition of about forty million
to the workforce, education and upgrading of skills will
continue to be major challenges. There will be heavy

demand for public healthcare. Provision of adequate water will be challenging and the effects of climate change will be daunting. The social consequences of all these will be serious. Most of these challenges fall in the domain of public policy, but the private sector cannot prosper if these issues are not satisfactorily resolved.

Third, Asia can become a global financial hub because of the large pool of capital supplied and demanded and the human skills in managing this capital. Until now, domestic or Asian regional financial markets have followed rather than led global finance. The dominant global financial institutions are still based in the United States and Europe. But their ownership could, over the years, change hands in favour of Asia.

Fourth, history shows that leadership in the global economy is firmly linked to leadership in thought and innovation. Although Japan has made significant techno-logical advances, Asia as a whole has yet to demonstrate strength in thought and innovation. Public policy and initiative is critical for this.

Fifth, while the size of economic and financial activity of a region or country is important in determining its position in the global economy, good governance is more important to command credibility and the confidence of global markets.

Sixth, intra-regional cooperation is already taking place on several fronts and in various forms. Notable initiatives in the recent past are a multilateral fund under the Chiang Mai Initiative, and an agreement for surveillance at the regional level (this initiative does not yet fully include India). To be effective in the global context, Asian regional cooperation may ultimately rest on four pillars: Japan, China, India and ASEAN.

Finally, history shows that major shifts in economic power in the world take place over a long period and may not be smooth. But technological development and globalization help expedite the process. Currently, a significant shift in global economic balance in favour of Asia is taking place.

Chapter 6 addresses some of the issues mentioned by placing them in a historical context, and poses some fundamental questions relating to the prospects for meaningful reforms, beyond what the authors describe as "tinkering with the financial system".

This book is indeed a valuable contribution to the literature on the subject and should enhance the quality of ongoing debates on the subject, among academicians, policy-makers and market participants.

Dr Yaga Venugopal Reddy
Former Governor of the Reserve Bank of India
December 2009

Preface

This book grew out of a series of articles I (the principal author) wrote and public lectures I gave in various parts of Asia in 2007 and 2008. As a matter of fact, when I gave one of my first lectures on the financial crisis in October 2007 at the Asian Development Bank (ADB), it did not attract much attention. As the Director General of the Private Sector Operations Department of the ADB was reported to have said, it (the crisis) was just a tempest in a teacup. In a later lecture I gave to the Bankers Association in Singapore in January 2008, I ended the talk by saying it was a perfect financial storm, and I was questioned about the validity of such a conclusion at that time. At the end of 2008, when the crisis was still raging, I was invited to speak at the Institute of Southeast Asian Studies, Singapore. After one of the talks, I was encouraged by the Director and the staff of the Institute to write a book on this subject. One of my good friends and tennis partner, Professor Lim Chin of the National University of Singapore, attended one of my lectures. During the height of the financial panic, he had separately written several articles and edited a book on the crisis. His offer to work with me on this book led to a fruitful partnership in this intellectual journey that has benefitted both of us.

In August 2007, a few weeks after the collapse of two hedge funds managed by Bear Stearns, reportedly the start of the great financial crisis, I started my research fellowship with the Asian Public Intellectuals (API) Programme of the Nippon Foundation. The topic of my research was the Asian financial crisis. I had spent twenty years as a banker in various international banks (Chemical Bank (now JP Morgan Chase), Credit Suisse First Boston, Deutsche Bank, Standard Chartered Bank and the Asian Development Bank). And prior to that I had done research on and taught political economy and sociology in various universities in the United States and Malaysia. When I left the field of banking and finance in 2007, I wanted to spend time to reflect and write on my experience in this area. The API programme offered me the opportunity to do just that, and the outbreak of the financial crisis just as I embarked on my research motivated to write not just about the Asian financial crisis but more importantly on the present crisis.

This book takes a multi-disciplinary approach to the great financial crisis of 2007–09. It combines the disciplines of economics, finance, sociology and politics to analyse the causes, consequences and challenges of the crisis. Above all it is historical and holistic in perspective. Too much of social science, in particular, the discipline of economics, has been dominated by an a-historical and fragmented way of thinking with disastrous consequences such that Paul Krugman, a recent Nobel laureate in Economics in his Lionel Robbins lecture in June 2009, stated that much of macroeconomics over the last few decades was useless at best and destructive at worst (Krugman 2009*b*).[1]

History is the basis of all social science because all social (economic included) phenomena have historical roots. Nothing emerges from nowhere. To comprehend the present forces and institutions, one has to understand the past, to discover how a particular phenomenon or problem originated and developed. To ignore history is to court ignorance and disaster. As George Santayana, the philosopher, puts it, "Those who cannot remember the past are condemned to repeat it." Or to rephrase it in a more positive way, the further one looks to the past, the more one can see forward.

The other approach that has been neglected in social science is a holistic and integrated understanding of social reality and the world. Science, like so much else, has become so specialized that every discipline has carved a niche for itself, with its own language, symbols and territorial turf. Most people have lost the ability to think holistically across disciplines; instead they are trapped in their silos-mentality. Capra (1983, p. 44), a physicist, wrote, "… overemphasis on the Cartesian method has led to the fragmentation that is characteristic of both our general thinking and academic disciplines, and to the widespread attitude of reductionism in science — the belief that all aspects of complex phenomena can be understood by reducing them to their constituent parts". As we shall show later, this fallacy of composition — reducing the whole to the sum of its parts — stands at the heart of the theoretical failure.

The great financial crisis is not the result of greedy financiers who took the world to the cleaners (that is a constant in the world of finance); or even simply the mistakes of central bankers and regulators who were caught asleep in their jobs, though they certainly share responsibility for the crisis. It is easier to look for convenient or accidental causes such as the lack of integrity of bankers,[2] or policy mistakes and poor implementation of policies, but more demanding intellectually and politically is to understand the underlying structural causes of the crisis. We propose that the causes of the crisis should be understood at three inter-related levels — the level of theory and ideology; the level of financial industry practices and malpractices that are a result of the failure of the theories; and finally the level structural imbalances in the international economy.

Chapter 1 begins with an analysis of the failure of the efficient market hypothesis and the rational expectations theory that underlie the disciplines of finance and macroeconomic theory. Rational expectations theorists believe market is always right in pricing assets, and government policies only reduce optimal allocation of resources. Blind faith in this assumption (it is no more than an assumption), has influenced not only academicians but more importantly policy-makers to adopt policies that accentuates financial instability. Chapter 2 traces the U.S. housing bubble that burst and triggered the financial crisis in relation to recent financial innovations that multiplied, rather than reduced, risks in the financial system. These included mortgage backed securities, collateralized debt obligation, credit default swaps, structured investment vehicles, private equity and leveraged buyouts.[3] Chapter 3 analyses how the financial industry in the United States became dominant again after almost fifty years of regulation, from the end of the Great Depression to the late 1970s. The re-emergence of finance over the real economy is associated with the rise in the ideology of deregulation and liberalization that escalated under President Reagan and Prime Minister Margaret

Thatcher. In the United States, the financial industry re-emerged with greater economic and political power after the bailout of the savings and loans crisis, and managed to capture the regulatory process over the years.

Chapter 4 moves beyond the financial industry to analyse structural changes in the U.S. economy that laid the foundation for the crisis. [In particular, the secular decline in the U.S. growth rate was counteracted by an increasingly debt-driven economy. Between 1960 and 2007, total debt in the U.S. economy rose 64 times compared to 27 times for its GDP. Financial debt exploded 490 times and household debt increased 64 times.] The imbalance between the financial sector and the real economy is the first structural imbalance. Two other structural imbalances explain the crisis — the wealth and income imbalance and the imbalance in current accounts between the United States and the rest of the world. [The relationship between wealth and income inequality and the financial crisis is crucial, yet systematically absent in most discussions on the crisis.] We argued that inequality led to overconsumption and the debt bubble for the majority, and over-savings and asset bubble for the minority in the United States. We also contend that wealth and income inequality plays a role in affecting current account imbalances by showing how it caused savings glut in China, while it, together with the growth of financial instruments and debt, caused a consumption glut in the U.S.

Chapter 5 discusses the impact of the crisis on Asian economies, its relation to the earlier Asian financial crisis, and the three major challenges facing Asia arising out of this crisis. They are the limits of the export-led growth model that has served Asia quite well, the issue of free capital flows and its destabilizing effects on the economies, and what, if any, alternatives Asia has to holding the U.S. dollar as the predominant international currency.

The final chapter closes by locating the crisis in a macro-historical perspective in terms of contestations in three realms. The crisis can be seen as a contest for continued hegemony by the United States in the international economic and financial system; a contest for continued dominance by the financial sector over the real economy; and finally, a contest of ideas between market fundamentalists and neo-liberals on the one hand and those who recognize the role of the state in human development on the other hand.

The crisis is an episode in these contestations. We have not seen the end of history, both in politics and in economics, as was proudly and prematurely asserted by neo-conservatives, such as Fukuyama, who touted the end of history after the fall of the Berlin Wall, and by mainstream economists, such as Bernanke, who spoke of the Great Moderation and the passing of business cycles. On the contrary, the future is uncertain.

To write a book, one has to stand on the shoulders of many. We owe much to friends and colleagues who have contributed in many ways to the formation of this book. In particular, we like to mention Dr Khor Hoe Ee, a long-time friend and former Assistant Managing Director of Economics at the Monetary Authority of Singapore. Dr Khor personally encouraged me to write my first paper on the financial crisis that was presented at the Federation of ASEAN Economists in Bangkok, December 2007. Subsequently we have had many discussions with him as the crisis unfolded and he also commented on parts of the manuscript. Others whose discussions we have benefitted from are Michael Anderson, James Miraflor, and Edsel Baja Jr. Thanks also go to Douglas Porpora, Chan Huan Chiang, Yilmaz Akyuz and Subramaniam Pillay who read and commented on sections of the draft manuscript. I was privileged to be able to tap on the knowledge of my former colleagues in banking and finance, particularly the helpful discussions with Charlie Chan, Victor Wee, Tan Kok Wee, Melissa Lee, Ananth Sankaran, and Siantoro Goeyardi on the complexities of financial products. This work would not be possible without the abled research assistance we received from the following persons — Liew Han Hsien, Chen Qun, Xylee Javier, and most of all, Stephen Santos who selflessly sacrificed much of his free time to assist us gather vital financial data. The authors also thank the external reviewers for their incisive comments, Triena Ong and Sheryl Sin for their editorial support and Fadzli Amir for the cover illustration. Finally, special thanks to Dr Venugopal Reddy, the former Governor of the Reserve Bank of India, who graciously agreed to write the Foreword and to share his insights on the issue. Last but not least, I am grateful to the Institute of Southeast Asian Studies for offering me a visiting fellowship to complete the manuscript.

The authors apologize to those who have contributed but whose names have been inadvertently missed. Needless to say, all shortcomings are the responsibility of the authors.

Michael Lim Mah-Hui
Penang
December 2009

Notes

1. Thirteen years earlier, in October 1998, one year after the Asian financial crisis started, Krugman wrote, "Suppose that you were to buy a copy of the best-selling textbook on international economics. What would it tell you about how to cope with such a sudden loss of confidence by international investors? Well, not much." He then added: "Trust me — I'm the coauthor of that textbook" (cited in Whalen 1999, footnote 13).

2. This is the argument made by Greenspan in his lecture at Georgetown University in October 2008 where he emphasized the lack of integrity of bankers as a major cause of the crisis. He said, those peddling derivatives were not as reliable as "the pharmacist who fills the prescription ordered by our physicians", and that in a market based on trust, he was "distressed how far we have let concerns for reputation slip in recent years" (cited in Goodman 2008).

3. Chapters 2, 3 and 4 are expansion of an earlier version of an article published as a working paper of the Levy Economics Institute. See Lim 2008.

1
The Power and Pitfalls of Theory

Introduction

There is nowhere to hide. What began as a crisis in the subprime sector ($2.5 trillion in size) of the U.S. housing industry in mid-2007 set the whole financial industry globally on fire and subsequently sucked the world economy into a global recession with growth rate of 3.1 per cent in 2008 and negative 1.4 per cent in 2009 (IMF 2009*b*). The implosion of the U.S. subprime mortgage industry has affected every asset class — from equities to bonds, from money markets to commodities; every type of credit — from mortgages to credit cards, to auto and student loans, to corporate debt and leveraged buy-outs; and every country that is integrated into the world financial system from Australia to Tokyo to Uzbekistan. The collapse of two Bear Stearns' hedge funds that invested in subprime collateralized debt obligations (CDOs) is the trigger of the crisis; it is not the cause.

The causes or origins of this crisis should be analysed at three inter-related levels — the theory and methodology underpinning the disciplines of neoclassical economics, finance and risk management; their influence on the evolution of the financial industry and poor regulatory practices; and the fundamental structural changes in the U.S. and international economy and the resulting major macroeconomic imbalances.

This chapter traces the roots of the crisis to the theoretical and methodological flaws in market efficiency theories that form the foundation of finance and risk management and how they contributed to the crisis.

Evolution of Macroeconomic Theory of Market Efficiency

Modern macroeconomics was born out of the Great Depression. In fact Ben Bernanke, the current Federal Reserve chairman, wrote in 1995 that "not only did the Depression give birth to macroeconomics as a distinct field of study, but ... the experience of the 1930's continues to influence macroeconomists' beliefs, policy recommendations, and research agendas" (cited in Koo 2008, p. xi). Keynes in "The General Theory of Employment, Interest, and Money" (1936, republished 1964), set out not only to explain the Depression but also constructed a new edifice for explaining the workings of, and interplay between the financial sector and the real economy. The Keynesian theory held sway for decades until the 1970s when it met difficulties in explaining the phenomenon of stagflation. It was then eclipsed by monetarists led by Milton Friedman whose views inspired a new generation of macroeconomic theorists led by Robert Lucas (1977), and Kydland and Prescott (1982), who began to reconstruct macroeconomics from the bottom up, beginning with the assumption that individuals with the right information will always act rationally, and concluding that their rational behaviour collectively contributes to an efficient market (see also Barbera 2009, p. 171ff). Furthermore, efficiency is attained whether the economy is riding through a boom or a bust of a business cycle. The key to an efficient market is therefore transparency in conveyance of information by the government and not government interference with aggregate demand management policies. Business cycles still exist in their model but only because of real shocks on the supply side, which is why it is called the Real Business Cycle (RBC) theory. Lucas, Kydland and Prescott received Nobel prizes for their elegantly constructed mathematical models, and the spirit of their message that the market is efficient even when we are riding through a business cycle, has a huge influence on the disciplines of finance and risk management, and also the policies and practices of central banks.

Modern financial theory is based on the belief in the efficient market hypothesis (EMH). The price of an asset, or its fair market value, is a result of an estimation of the present value of its future income stream based on a constant stream of information. Every decision to buy or sell reflects a judgment on the future income stream and the discount rate; these information change every moment and are captured in the myriad of data provided by all types of data sources. As data change, market prices likewise change. "The key message of the Efficient Market Hypothesis is that asset prices are *always and everywhere* at the correct price. That is to say, today's market prices, no matter what they are, correctly reflect assets' true values ..." (Cooper 2008, italics original). Capital markets are believed to be efficient because they price risks and returns correctly. There is no room for asset price bubbles as extreme price swings are simply markets responding to new information and changing conditions. Markets when left alone will always converge to a steady equilibrium state; and markets are the most efficient method for allocation of resources. Hence markets should be given a free rein to determine prices and resource allocation; government and other external forces are considered interferences that result in suboptimal states. For traders, this means they cannot consistently outperform the markets except through luck; and for central banks, it means they should not interfere in price movements in assets markets because regulators know less than markets and markets are always correctly priced by conditions underlying demand and supply.

Influence of Efficient Market Hypothesis on Policy

This faith in the efficiency of financial markets has significant influence over policy-making among central bankers. Foremost among these are central bankers like Alan Greenspan who believe market prices are efficient, hence they do not want to second-guess markets, and are reluctant to take a position to cool markets even when they exhibit irrational exuberance. The original role of the central banking system in America after the Great Depression was to safeguard financial stability by managing the credit creation system. Over time and with the introduction of fiat money it began to focus primarily on containing wage and consumer price inflation. Significantly, the Federal

Reserve Bank ("Fed") is interested in taming consumer price inflation and not asset price inflation; the latter was deemed outside their purview. Financial markets are considered side shows when they are, in fact, central to the repeated booms and busts experienced. This neglect is a major contributory factor in build up of asset bubbles. Yet, these same people who believe markets are efficient when there is a bubble, do not believe in market efficiency when there is a bust. Somehow markets are not pricing assets efficiently when prices are spirally downward. Central banks and governments scramble to intervene in the markets — to prop up prices because markets have mispriced them. Interest rates are dropped, credit creation expanded, quantitative easing introduced, and accounting principles, such as mark-to-market rules, are suspended or modified.

Challenges to Efficient Market Hypothesis

The EMH has been subjected to criticisms by behavioural economists who attribute market imperfections to human errors in reasoning and information (Kahneman et al. 1982; Thaler and de Bondt 1985). Empirical evidence in support of EMH had also been mixed. Most notably, Shiller (2000) argued that the dotcom stock market was overvalued and that eventually crashed in the month the book was published. The second edition of the book, published in 2005, was updated to cover the U.S. housing bubble. In it Shiller presciently warned the housing bubble would burst which eventually occurred in 2007. More recently, George Cooper (2008) has articulated a stronger and more fundamental criticism of the EMH by proposing the hypothesis that financial markets, unlike goods markets, are inherently unstable.[1]

Challenges to Financial Risk Management

A major methodological assumption of the EMH and risk management theory is that individual price movements are random and unpredictable, like the outcome of a coin toss; but the probability of distribution of outcomes is predictable, and resembles a Gaussian-type normal distribution. In the physical world, such well-behaved randomness is fairly non-controversial. However, in the complex social world, and especially in financial markets where human psychology, animal spirit, fear and greed rein, and where self-reinforcing feedback impacts future outcomes, this assumption is questionable at best and naïve at worst.[2]

In financial markets, repeated booms and busts do not square with the theory of convergence to market equilibrium; the distribution of risks often are not normal distribution but exhibit fat-tail[3] distributions where extreme events are found at the tails of the distribution. What is considered very unlikely to occur in say a five standard deviation scenario under a normal curve is actually less unlikely in a fat-tail curve. The collapse of Long Term Capital Management in 1998 and AIG Financial Product in 2008 illustrate this problem poignantly. According to Long Term Capital Management's chief financial officer, the firm suffered from adverse "25 standard deviation events several days in a row" — something that should not have happened under a normal distribution scenario (Cooper 2008, pp. 10–11).

There are many who believe that the problem with risk management models is not methodological but empirical, i.e., the historical data used for estimating the future risks do not go back far enough. They only capture information in times of financial stability. Hence, Greenspan in his testimony to Congress in 2008, stated, "... because the data inputted into the risk management models covered a period of euphoria. Had ... the models been fitted more appropriately to historic periods of stress, capital requirements would have been much higher and the financial world would be in far better shape today." (Barbera 2009, p. 184).

But others like Cooper (2008) believe that the problem is deeper and more fundamental. In the field of statistics, Knightian uncertainty refers to the problem where neither the individual outcome nor the distribution of outcomes can be known. Risk management tries to eliminate this uncertainty through the collection and analysis of historical data. But the inherent instability in financial systems, the recursive or positive feedback effects in market (memory effect) and clustering effect (bunching of extreme movements in short time period) all work to render risk management techniques based on normal distribution unreliable (Cooper 2008, pp. 145–53). He further argues that financial markets, unlike consumer goods markets, do not always follow the normal laws of demand and supply; in fact, they often behave contrary to these laws. In consumer goods markets, when price rises, demand drops, and when price drops, demand increases.

Likewise, when price rises, supply increases and when price drops, supply declines. The intersection of the supply and demand curves results in price equilibrium. This model is extrapolated onto financial markets where the behaviour of consumers in financial markets is quite different from that in consumption goods markets; such behaviour are driven more by speculation and expectations of future returns that are essentially unknown than by the satisfaction of human needs. There is a limit to the latter but the former is insatiable. The more money one accumulates, the more one wants. The more one sees others accumulate, the greater the urge to emulate. Kindleberger (2000, p. 15) astutely observed, "There is nothing so disturbing to one's well-being and judgment as to see a friend get rich." Herd mentality, greed and fear play more important roles than rational expectation theories care to admit. It can be observed that, more often than not, when the price of financial assets like stock rises, demand, instead of falling, increases. Buyers, expecting or betting on future gains chase after the stocks sending them higher until a bubble is formed and correction occurs. Likewise, when price of stock falls, investors sell on fears and worries until a correction takes place. The experience of a great scientist and genius like Issac Newton shows how little we have learned or moved. In 1730, he wrote, "I can calculate the motions of the heavenly bodies, but not the madness of men." A while later, he sold his shares in the South Sea Company for a tidy profit of 7,000 pounds only to re-enter the market, with a larger bet when the going was too good, to ultimately lose 20,000 pounds. It is said he never wanted to hear the word South Sea Company again (Kindleberger 2000, p. 31).

In short, modern mainstream finance and risk management theories are based on tenuous assumptions and methods where empirical data may not fit the theories. By believing that they can anticipate and price in risks accurately, these risk management tools sometimes have the disastrous consequence of luring market into a false sense of security (Cooper 2008, p. 128). The result is for market participants to pile up huge amounts of risks with the false confidence that they and the system can handle these risks. Typical of such hubris is the statement by Joe Anderson, a high ranking executive of Country-wide Mortgage which was once the largest mortgage lender in the U.S. until it went bankrupt in 2007: "We have a wealth of information we didn't have before. We understand the data and can price the risk" (Farzad et al. 2007).

Ideological Crisis

The power and ramifications of theories and ideas on daily life cannot be underestimated. Theory and academia provide powerful underpinnings to policies and practices because practitioners can claim to have "scientific" foundation to their practices. To the extent that neoclassical economists, monetarists, and rational expectation theorists have dominated and guided business, finance and economic thinking the last few decades, they have contributed to the present financial and economic crisis and are themselves facing an intellectual crisis, so that no less than Greenspan admitted that "… the whole intellectual edifice collapsed" (*Economist* 2009c, p. 83).

Alternative Paradigm — The Financial Instability Hypothesis

In contrast to the neoclassical and efficient market hypothesis view of markets, Keynes (1964) and Minsky (1986), hold a different view. For them, there are inherent forces in markets, both psychological and structural, that make markets, particularly financial markets, inherently unstable rather than converge towards equilibrium. Markets often do not always allocate resources efficiently; booms and busts are part of capitalist growth. Rather than viewing government as external forces interfering with market's optimal allocation of resources, government play important roles in managing the excesses of markets.

Since investment decisions necessarily involve taking a view of the future with expectations of future profits, uncertainty is inherent in every investment decision (Burkett and Wohar 1987). In contrast, market efficiency economists assume the future can be treated as a matter involving risk reducible to the calculation of probabilities (Whalen 2009, p. 5). Keynes explicitly rejected the substitution of uncertainty with calculable risks and the focus on long periods of equilibrium by classical economists.

As he wrote

> The whole subject of the accumulation of wealth is to produce results, or potential results, at a comparatively distant, and sometimes at an indefinitely distant date. Thus the fact that our knowledge of the future is fluctuating, vague and uncertain renders wealth a peculiarly unsuitable subject for the methods of

classical economic theory. This theory might work well in a world in which economic goods were necessarily consumed within a short interval of their being produced. But it requires, I suggest, considerable amendment if it is to be applied to a world in which the accumulation of wealth for an indefinitely postponed future is an important factor … (cited in Whalen 2009, p. 5)

Minsky built on the foundation of Keynes and understood financial systems as swinging from periods of overconfidence and stability to periods of despair and panic. In fact, the seeds of every crisis are sown in times of stability where overconfidence and underestimation of risks convince people to taking excessive risks to the point when small disappointments trigger devastating consequences.

Based on Minsky's paradigm, Kindleberger's (2000) study on the history of financial crisis from 1600s to 1990s suggested an anatomy of a typical financial crisis that starts with displacement, that is, change from external sources, leading to euphoria, excessive speculation and bubble, and eventually any small disappointments will produce distress, panic and crash, and eventual recovery (see Figure 1.1). The present financial crisis fits well into this anatomy. Displacement came in the form of deregulation beginning in the late 1970s that spurred financial innovations in the 1980s till 2000s. This fertile environment aided by loose monetary policies, capital inflows, and relatively long periods of economic stability (low inflation) led to overconfidence and underestimation of risks. Financial derivatives enabled the financial system to take on more

FIGURE 1.1
Anatomy of Financial Crisis

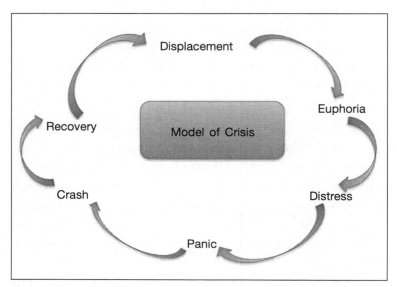

risks thinking that the risks have been passed on to others in the system. Finally, the asset bubble that was built up imploded when small disappointments (defaults in subprime mortgage sector) produced distress (collapse of Bear Stearns' hedge funds), panic (generalized credit and liquidity crunch), and crash (collapse of Lehman Brothers, AIG and the whole credit market), leading to eventual bailout by governments throughout the world.

Unlike rational expectation theories that analyse economic and financial systems based on individual components, in this case, the rational decisions in individual actors, the alternative paradigm of financial instability of Minsky, is more structural, historical and holistic. It avoids the fallacy of composition of rational expectation theories where the whole is analysed in terms of the sum of its parts. The fallacy of composition refers to the idea of mistaking the whole as simply the sum of its parts. Rational expectation theorists assume every individual makes rational economic decisions based on full information, and collectively these produce a stable and efficient equilibrium for the system as a whole. But in fact, the opposite can, and does, happen. Every individual making rational decision from his or her own vantage point, can contribute to systemic instability and failure. The tragedy of commons, the paradox of thrift, the idea of maximization of profit without regard to consequences on society are examples of the fallacy of composition where every individual making rational decisions in his or her own interest can lead to a dysfunctional system. As we shall demonstrate in greater detail in Chapter 3, under the Economic Value Added (EVA) School, the maximization of shareholders value when applied to banks produced the imperative for each bank to maximize its return on capital. This is achieved through various means such as increasing leverage (minimizing use of the bank's own capital), shedding activities that require higher capital requirements, such as traditional lending, in favour of investment banking activities like securitization and trading that consume less capital requirement. Thus even while the risks of individual banks may be reduced, collectively, the systemic risks are multiplied.

While the concept of fallacy of composition is not new, it is nevertheless ignored or neglected in theories of rational expectations and efficient market, with significant impact on policy-making so that regulators thought that it was enough only to regulate the risks of individual banks to produce a healthy banking system. After this crisis, Summers recognized that "a change in conceptual approach from [one] based on the fallacy of composition — that in regulating each individual entity for its own health you are regulating the whole system — to [one] based on what is necessary for system stability" (Guha 2009).

stage theory Finally, Minsky, in the tradition of economists like Marx, Schumpeter and Keynes, analysed the cyclicality of financial crisis in the context of the structural evolution of capitalist economy — one that has moved from merchant capitalism, to industrial capitalism, to financial (money-manager) capitalism (Whalen 1999). Structural questions — necessarily missing from rational expectation and market efficiency theories, such as changes in the structure of an economy, changes in the financial structure and its relative position in the economy, the degree of mix in the types of financing (from hedge, to speculative, to Ponzi financing) in the economy, the relation of intense competition between banks to maximize profits, the balance of economic and political power between those in business and finance and the public — are more important for understanding the workings of the financial system than simply the aggregation of decisions of individual rational actors. Analysing the economy from this structural and historical perspective, Minsky concluded that, far from slipping into oblivion, financial crisis have become more frequent and accentuated with the dominance of finance over the real economy.

The next chapter examines the practices and mal-practices in the financial industry and the myriad of financial innovations over the last few decades that have contributed to the crisis.

Notes

1. This discussion on the flaws in efficient market hypothesis is based on the work of Cooper (2008). See also Crotty (2008).
2. These traits were recognized and given emphasis by Keynes (1964) and Minsky (1986) in their theories and analyses. More recently, Shiller and Akerlof have also emphasized their role in explaining excesses in financial behaviour (Shiller 2009a).
3. Under a normal distribution curve, events that deviate from the mean by five standard deviations are extremely rare and those that are ten or more standard deviations away are considered almost impossible. But under a fat tail distribution such occurrences are less rare; this has been borne out in several incidences in financial markets disasters.

2
Financial Innovations and Industry Practices

The U.S. Housing Market

The financial crisis started in July 2007 when the U.S. housing mortgage party ended. Investment and mortgage bankers made millions, some billions, from the party. Wall Street took in $27 billion in revenue from selling and trading asset backed securities (Farzad 2007). Many middle class families saw their home equity rise and felt rich. Even those from lower classes "benefited" temporarily. They were able to own houses with minimal down payment and move into new houses, but not for long. As house prices rose, they borrowed more on home equity. Everyone was having a good time. No one wanted to take the punch bowl away, certainly not Greenspan. Median house prices in the U.S. shot up 40 per cent between 2000 and 2006 to a high of $234,000. The ratio of median house price to median household income rose from a historically stable ratio of three times (from 1970–2000) to five times in 2006 (Leonhardt 2007). See Figure 2.1. The ratio of median house price to rental income increased from 100 per cent to 160 per cent between 2000 and 2006 (Krugman 2009a, p. 145ff). As early as 2006, some economists have warned that this euphoria was unsustainable (Papadimitriou et al. 2006). See Figure 2.2.

FIGURE 2.1
Ratio of Median House Price to Median Household Income

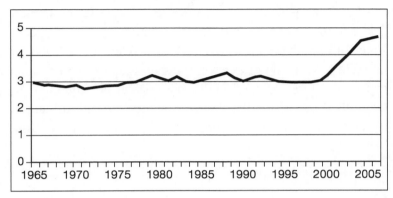

Source: Leonhardt (2007).

FIGURE 2.2
Ratio of House Price to Rental Income

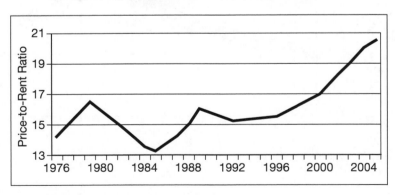

Source: Papadimitriou et al. (January 2006).

House prices tapered off and started to decline by middle of 2006 and fell sharply in 2007 and 2008.

Figure 2.3 shows the Case-Shiller Home Price Indices for the Composite 10 and Composite 20 cities in the United States. The Composite-10 index reached a peak of 226 in June 2006 and has declined to 162 in December 2008. It has fallen over 30 per cent on the average with some areas in excess of 50 per cent and may fall further till 2010 to bring the ratio of median house price to household income to sustainable levels (Shiller 2009*b*). With a $20 trillion

FIGURE 2.3
Case-Shiller Home Price Index, U.S., 2000–08

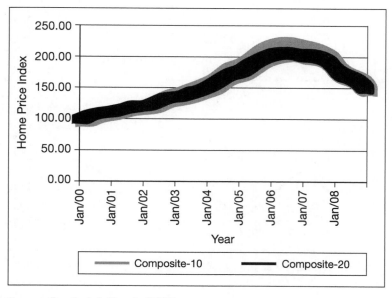

Source: Standard & Poor's (2009).

housing sector, every 10 per cent fall shaves off $2 trillion in household wealth. Concomitantly, default and foreclosure rates began to climb. In 2006, 1.2 million household loans were foreclosed, up 42 per cent from the previous year. It is estimated that two million homes were foreclosed in 2007 and even more in 2008 when 2.5 million adjustable rate mortgages reset higher (Schwartz 2007; Callan 2007). The rate of home delinquency (thirty days and above) rose from 6.7 per cent in December 2006 to 23 per cent in December 2008 and the rate of foreclosure jumped from 1.6 per cent to 7.6 per cent over the same period (Tanzi 2009). More than 8 million mortgages (one in 10) have negative equity and U.S. household wealth has been reduced by $13.3 trillion (about 100 per cent of GDP) by end of 2008 (World Bank 2009, p. 37).

How did house prices build up such an excess bubble? Excess liquidity, i.e., cheap and plentiful money is a necessary condition for asset price bubbles. In this case, the combination of the Fed dropping its interest rate from over 6 per cent in 2000 to 1 per cent in 2003 to push the economy out of a recession following the dotcom bubble further fanned the property bubble. Professor John Taylor of Stanford University blamed the Fed for loose monetary policies between 2002 and the end of 2004 (Wolf 2007*b*). He argued that interest rates should have risen from the low of 1.75 per cent in 2001 to 5.25 per cent in 2005 rather than it being pushed down to 1 per cent in 2003 and then raising it slowly (*Economist* 2007*d*). See Figure 2.4. The Bank of England pursued the same loose monetary policy and egged on the UK housing boom and price inflation with further rate cuts in 2005.

FIGURE 2.4

U.S. Federal Fund Rate and the Taylor Rule

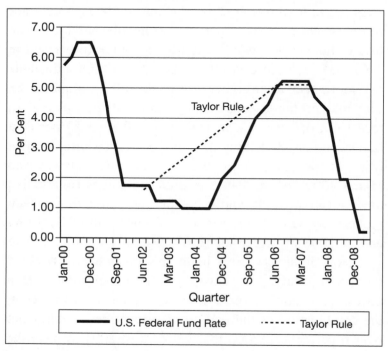

Source: Scheuble (2009).

The rise in house prices and purchasing power was an antidote to the $7 trillion losses suffered in the stock market crash in the dotcom crisis. Another factor at work is what is now known as the Greenspan conundrum, i.e., even though Greenspan raised interest rates gradually after 2004, long-term interest rates stayed low due to the excess liquidity provided by inflow of foreign funds, particularly from Asia. While there was excess liquidity on the supply side, it was matched by excesses in financial innovations on the demand side. Just as in consumer goods where demand can be created through advertising, demand for credit in financial markets can also be created and sustained through all types of financial innovations that magnified the systemic risks of the financial system, though at that time many, such as Greenspan, were singing praises of how the risks have been dispersed and tamed.[1]

The complacency towards risk by so many players in the financial market that eventually led to a massive build up of systemic risk is best explained by Minsky (1986) who wrote that stability breeds instability, i.e., long periods of economic growth and success create overconfidence in the system. Businessmen and investors expand production and believe in rosy forecasts, bankers and financiers reduce risk premium and margins of safety in good times, markets underestimate and underprice risks in periods of financial stability. As he put it: "Whenever full employment is achieved and sustained, business and bankers, heartened by success, tend to accept larger doses of financing. During periods of tranquil expansion, profit-seeking financial institutions invent and reinvent 'new' forms of money, substitutes for money in portfolios, and financing techniques for various types of activity; financial innovation is a characteristics of our economy in good times" (cited in Barbera 2009, p. 7). The types of financial innovations he wrote about in the early 1980s such as the introduction of commercial paper market, the use of new forms of short-term funding other than deposits are staid

and safe by today's standards. Financial innovations that
he did not anticipate began to emerge. The most important
of these is the securitization of debt.

Financial Innovations

Mortgage Backed Securities (MBS)

One of the most important changes in the financial
landscape is the introduction of securitization of assets,
beginning with house mortgages in the early 1980s.
Until then, loans that banks originated sat on their books
until they matured and were paid off. In the early 1980s,
financial engineers started to package bank loans into
securities that could be bought and sold, known as asset
backed securities (ABS). The most common ABS, based on
home mortgages, is known as mortgage backed securities
(MBS). The securitization of housing mortgages into MBS
has enabled banks and mortgage companies to increase
the velocity and turnover of loans as banks and mortgage
companies securitized, sold off these loans and booked more
new loans. This is known as the "origination-distribution"
model. The volume of MBS originated and traded reached
$3 trillion in 2005 in a U.S. housing mortgage industry
of $10 trillion (Farzad et al. 2007, p. 33). Securitization
enabled banks and mortgage companies, the originators
of these loans, to take on more loans as they moved
the securitized loans off their books. In fact, mortgage
companies and real estate developers who entered the fray
have overshadowed banks that were the traditional home
loan providers. Many large housing developers aggressively

pushed mortgages to borrowers in order to boost sales. For example, Pulte Home, the country's largest developer by market capitalization provided mortgages for 90 per cent of the houses they built. These new players have neither the credit skills nor the interest to conduct proper due diligence of potential homebuyers. Their interest is in pushing out the houses as fast as they are built. The MBS instruments allowed all these institutions to transfer the risks to other investors. The dissociation of ownership of assets from risks encouraged poor credit assessment and was fundamental in reducing the margin of safety and increasing the margin of risks.

Subprime mortgages simply mean lending to house borrowers with weak credit. Lenders did so by providing teasers like minimal or zero down payment, and low introductory adjustable rate mortgages, as well as lax documentation and credit checks. Between 2004 and 2006, $1.5 trillion (15 per cent of the total U.S. housing loans) of subprime mortgages were booked (Brooks and Mitchell 2007). Total subprime loans form 25 per cent of the housing mortgage market (Capell 2007); these subprime loans were fine as long as the housing market continued to boom and interest rates did not rise. When these conditions disappeared, the first to default were subprime borrowers. These defaults caused an implosion of the mortgage backed securities (MBS) and the collateralized debt obligations (CDOs) industry. The blow out surfaced in June 2007 with the collapse of two subprime mortgage hedge funds managed by Bear Stearns, quickly followed by the suspension of three other funds managed by BNP Paribas.

Collateralized Debt Obligations (CDOs)

In the early 1990s, financial innovation took these MBS to a higher level in terms of complexity and leverage with the introduction of collateralized debt obligations (CDOs). They are simply the bundling of a class of asset backed securities into a special purpose vehicle and then rearranging these assets into different tranches with different credit ratings, interest rate payments, and priority of repayment. For example, a CDO could consist of 100 subprime mortgage backed securities (MBS). Using historical rates of default and recovery, let us assume that in an extreme case of default, the loss ratio is no more than 10 per cent. These subprime MBS are then divided into AAA tranche (70 per cent), mezzanine tranche (20 per cent), and subordinated tranche (10 per cent). An investor, depending on his risk appetite, can choose which tranche to invest in. The AAA tranche pays lowest interest rate, but provides highest priority in terms of debt repayment. A graphic illustration of a CDO would look like that in Figure 2.5

FIGURE 2.5

Structure of a Basic Collateralized Debt Obligation (CDO)

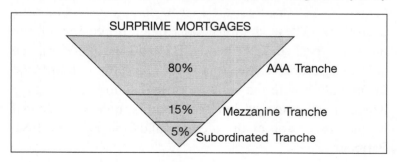

To further complicate matters, these CDOs were used as underlying assets and repackaged to the next level of CDOs. This is referred to as CDO squared and after another round, it becomes CDO cubed. Layered on top of these are CDOs of CDSs (credit default swaps) that multiplied the risks further. The defaults are confined not only to the underlying securities but also the contracts written (CDS) on the traded securities. Often these CDOs cross hold each other. The higher the level of CDO, the more removed it is from the actual underlying security, complicating the pricing of these CDOs. The volume of CDOs issued tripled between 2004 and 2007 from \$150 billion to \$544 billion per year. See Figure 2.6.

FIGURE 2.6
Worldwide CDO Issues, 2000–June 2009

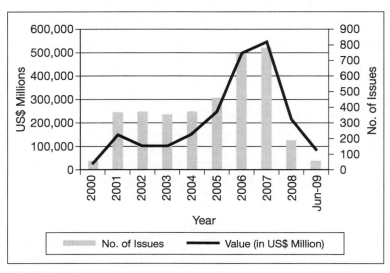

Source: Bloomberg.

These CDOs were distributed far and wide. Not only banks throughout the world, but also staid establishments such as town councils in far flung places like Australia and Norway that were chasing for higher yields, bought these CDOs. Bank of China alone is exposed to $9 billion of subprime CDOs. Two German state banks investing in CDOs went bankrupt and had to be bailed out by the government. A recent estimate of Asian financial institutions' exposure to subprime-related losses put it at $23.4 billion, of which $11.1 billion are from Japanese institutions (Yap and Pierson 2009).

These CDOs resemble a house built on a deck of cards; when the cards slip, the house falls apart. As subprime borrowers began to default, investors in the subordinate tranche of the subprime CDOs took the first hit. This led to a loss of confidence even among investors in the safer tranches who had not suffered any losses. Panic ensues as they head for the exit door together. The fire sale of assets led to a downward spiral of prices and a freeze in funding for these CDOs.

Leverage and Mismatch

To add fuel to fire, many of these transactions were done on a leveraged and mismatched basis. Leverage, in layman's terminology, is using other people's money. Leverage and maturity mismatch are basic tools of banks and financial institutions. Banks are nothing but financial intermediaries, i.e., they gather savings from people and institutions who do not need to use the savings for a period of time, and lend them to individuals and institutions who are in need, and in the process make an interest rate spread. Because there is a difference in timing for the use of funds between depositors and borrowers, banks are able to take advantage of this to lend out more than the deposits they gather from borrowers. This gives rise to the phenomena of leverage and maturity mismatch. Traditionally, banks are required to maintain a capital adequacy ratio of 8 per cent. This means they should keep 8 per cent of their balance sheet in the form of their own capital; the rest are borrowed money. In this case, the leverage is twelve times. Typically banks borrow mainly from depositors; hence deposits form over 70 per cent of a bank's balance sheet, the rest they borrow from institutions and money markets or bond markets. Borrowings by banks in the form of deposits are relatively stable where as borrowings from large institutional investors are unstable sources of funds that increase vulnerability to run on banks.

Maturity mismatch, sometimes termed short funding, refers to the different maturity term between a bank's assets and liabilities. Banks typically borrow short term and lend longer term, i.e., its liabilities are of shorter maturity than its assets. For example, a bank takes in savings deposits that can be withdrawn anytime, or one-month fixed deposits, and provides loans to its customers who normally borrow for longer periods. Since yield curves (the difference in interest rates between short- and long-term debt) are normally positive, with short-term debt yielding lower interest than long-term debt, banks make a profit in the interest differential; the larger the interest rate differential, the steeper the yield curve, and the smaller the interest rate differential, the gentler the slope.

Sometimes, yield curves become negative — in this case short-term interest rates become higher than long-term rates. Banks and financial institutions run into trouble when this occurs, as in the case of the U.S. savings and loans crisis in the later 1980s, because they are paying out more on their liabilities than they are earning from their assets. Instead of making a gain, they make a loss. Even when yield curves are positive, banks can still run into trouble with short funding. When banks borrow short term in the money market, say on thirty days basis, they are exposed to the risks of having to re-finance their debt every month. What if investors refuse to refinance? They have to borrow from other sources or sell their assets to repay the investors. What if the proceeds from the assets sold are inadequate to repay the investors? They are forced to sell more assets or to borrow from other sources.

In short, banks and financial institutions have to manage their assets and liabilities judiciously to avoid financial disaster.

But they did just the opposite over the last few decades, especially non-bank financial institutions like investment banks, hedge funds, private equity funds and even some money market and mutual funds. These financial institutions over leveraged and over mismatched. The average leverage (total assets to equity ratio) of top five investment banks in the U.S. rose from 12 times to 30 times between 2000 and 2007. At a leverage of 30 times, the margin of safety of a bank is razor-thin. All it takes is a fall in value of over 3 per cent of its assets and the bank is technically insolvent (the value of its liabilities are greater than its assets). Leverage for hedge funds are notoriously high and could reach one hundred times. Even deposit-taking banks, particularly the universal banks in the U.S. that combine commercial and investment banking activities, jacked up their leverage to 20 times. For example, the leverage of Citibank went from 12 times in 2000 to 19 times in 2007. It is reported that if the on and off-balance sheet liabilities are added, the leverage of Citigroup reached 88 times (Ferguson 2008).

Leveraging is one sure way of making high profits. In fact, the less of your own money you use, the higher the return. It is, therefore, no surprise that financial institutions that are in the position to leverage make the highest returns. This explains in large part the disproportionate share of total corporate profits that has flowed to the financial sector (30 per cent) compared to the manufacturing sector (21 per cent) in the U.S. See Figure 3.2. Leverage is exhilarating when prices are going up; it is devastating when prices are heading down. In fact, what begins as a trickle turns into a torrent as institutions begin to sell their assets putting more pressure on prices. One round of selling leads to another until in extreme cases, there is simply no market left which is what we witnessed in the depth of the crisis for almost every asset class.

Credit Crunch Spreads to Other Sectors

Conduits and Structured Investment Vehicles (SIVs)

What began as a credit squeeze in the subprime mortgage sector quickly spreads to other areas, particularly to conduits and leveraged buy-out (LBO) transactions initially, and later, to monoline bond insurers, credit default swaps, and rippling out to consumer loans (credit cards and auto loans).

Conduits and SIVs have become a large part of the banking industry. Banks set up conduits as special-purpose vehicles to hold assets such as MBS or CDOs for their clients in exchange for hefty fees. While banks do not own or control these conduits, they are exposed to them through the provision of back-up credit lines to these conduits. Because these exposures are off-balance sheets, banks are able to circumvent the capital adequacy ratio. To further muddy the waters, most conduits are set up in tax haven territories to avoid tax and to circumvent banking regulations and governance. Conduits engage in funding mismatch, i.e., they borrow short term in the commercial paper market to invest in long-term, higher yielding assets like CDOs and MBS. The size of the conduit market is huge although there is no accurate way to gauge it. Citibank disclosed in its second quarter of 2007 results that it had $77 billion of assets and liabilities in conduits. JP Morgan had issued $54 billion in commercial paper for conduits. Of the $3 trillion global commercial paper market, banks provided $1.1 trillion of back-up credit lines to conduits (Reilly and Mollenkamp 2007).

In other words, since these conduits can draw on the banks' credit lines, the risks that went out the front door have found their way back through the back door. This is the primary reason why the money market froze up in September 2007. Banks were hoarding cash to meet their credit obligations in case the conduits knocked on their doors. Hence, despite the European Central Bank

(ECB) and the Fed pumping in close to $100 billion of liquidity into the system, the LIBOR rate climbed to a high of 6.88 per cent (Giles 2007*a*). In December 2007, five central banks launched a coordinated effort to pump in hundreds of billions of liquidity into the banking system to calm the money market (Giles 2007*b*).

Leveraged Buy-Out (LBO)

Leveraged buy-outs (LBOs), usually associated with private equity funds, have exploded in recent years. Private equity funds are closely held by high net worth individuals and large institutions that are not listed on stock exchanges. They are set up as partnerships to minimize taxes; they are unregulated, have no disclosure requirements, and are often established in tax haven territories.

In an era of loose credit, excess liquidity, and rising asset prices, these funds were able to mobilize billions of dollars from the rich as well as institutions such as pension funds, insurance companies, university endowment funds, and government investment vehicles. Private equity funds raised $232 billion in 2005, $459 billion in 2006, and $240 billion in the first half of 2007 (Berman 2007; Economist 2007*b*).

The huge capital at their disposal gives them clout in the market to borrow many times over their capital base to take over companies. These transactions are known as LBOs. The size of recent LBOs are mind boggling: $32 billion for TXU, a Texas utility company; $26 billion for First Data, a credit card processor; $49 billon for BCE, a Canadian telecoms provider (Berman 2007; *Economist*

2007*b*). Typically, in LBO private equity funds put up less than 30 per cent of the money themselves. The rest is borrowed from banks and investors through the issuance of collateralized loan obligations.

The most recent wave of LBOs was fuelled by cheap credit and excess liquidity. From 2003 to the first half of 2007, $13.3 trillion (equivalent to the GDP of the United States) of LBOs were booked, with $2.7 trillion alone in the first half of 2007, accounting for 37 per cent of all investment banking transactions. After the subprime mortgage crisis, LBO deals plummeted to $222 billion in August 2007, compared to $579 billion in July and $695 billion in April of the same year (Berman 2007). See Figure 2.7. Many of these LBOs were funded by bridge loans from banks. Banks have over $300 billion of these bridge

FIGURE 2.7

Global Merger and Acquisition Transactions, 2005–09

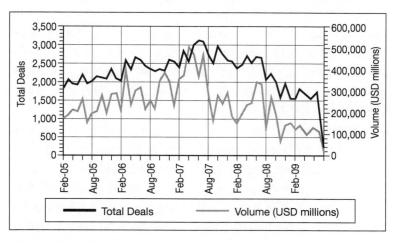

Source: Bloomberg.

loans that they have difficulty selling or have to sell at a discount (Politi 2007; Ng 2007). Deutsche Bank's chief executive officer, Ackermann, called on banks to value these securities transparently to restore market confidence (Larsen and Simensen 2007). By early October 2007, investment and commercial banks lined up to announce their losses. Big players like Citibank, Merrill Lynch, UBS, and Deutsche Bank posted close to $20 billion in losses for their third quarter results (Enrich 2007; Singer et al. 2007; Taylor E. 2007). Three months later, many of these same banks had to more than double their initial write down. Banks like Merrill Lynch, Citibank, and UBS posted losses of close to $20 billion each.

Because of the size of LBO deals and the high level of leverage, defaults in the LBO market will be more destabilizing to the financial market than defaults in the subprime mortgage market. It was estimated that the recovery rate for distressed LBOs of the early 2000s was about 75 per cent. Between 2004 and 2007, the leverage (debt to operating profit) of acquired companies rose from 4.8 times to 7.0 times, while their debt servicing capacity (operating profit to debt repayment) fell from 3.4 times to 1.8 times (Farzad et al. 2007, p. 34). Some individual deals have leverages as high as ten times. Such high leverage is inherently risky in the face of a decline in credit cycle or missed targets in business plans. Rating companies are expecting a rise in corporate defaults and reviewing hundreds of thousands of bond issues and leveraged transactions (Cookson et al. 2008; Saft 2008). The Boston Consulting Group estimates that half of the companies owned by private equity funds may default in the next three years leading to losses of $300 billion or more of which $50 billion to $80 billion may be borne by banks (*Economist* 2009*b*).

Lax credit criteria found in subprime loans are repeated in LBO deals. Until August 2007, banks offered goodies to borrowers in the form of "covenant lite" loans (i.e., banks waived traditional monitoring rights and financial covenants), and payment-in-kind notes (borrower need not pay in cash but in kind using another credit note). In other words, debt is piled upon debt. A new covenant known as "you snooze, you loose" is introduced into LBO deals (i.e., lenders who did not reply when borrowers request for changes in loan covenants are deemed to have given their consent). Many LBO deals struck in the first half of 2007 are now delayed or renegotiated after investors lost their appetite for them, prompting law suits against banks who underwrote the deals (Cimilluca and Enrich 2007).

A comparison of subprime loans with LBO loans reveals that they share many similar features and both can be classified as Ponzi financing schemes in the framework of Minsky. Building on Keynes, Minsky (1986) observed that financial stability and fragility is essentially determined by the margin of safety (the ability of banks to convert assets to meet cash demands), and the ability of borrowers to meet their debt obligations from cash flow.

He identified three types of financing — hedge financing, speculative financing, and Ponzi financing. Hedge financing refers to lending whereby the expected cash flow from operations of the borrower is adequate to meet both interest and principal repayments. This would be traditional bank lending based on the financial strength of a borrower to repay both interest and principal from its cash flow from operation. Speculative financing is more risky; here a borrower's cash flow is able to meet interest payment but not necessary principal repayment. Speculative financing involves the rolling over of maturing debt. Again in bank lending, it is not uncommon for principal to be rolled over, as in an "evergreen" loan. But banks test the financial strength of a borrower by requiring it to periodically repay its principal for a short time, a process known as cleaning up the loan. Ponzi financing, the most risky, is where a borrower's cash flow is inadequate to meet interest payment, let alone principal repayment. Lenders expect part of repayment to come from refinancing, increase in collateral value and/or debt, and sale of assets. The fragility of a financial system is then dependent on the mix of these forms of financing. The more a financial system depends on speculative and Ponzi financing, the greater its fragility. As he noted, "An increase in the ratio of Ponzi finance, so that it is no longer a rare event, is an indicator that the fragility of the financial structure is in a danger zone for a debt-deflation" (Minsky 1986, p. 341).

Using the above definitions, subprime mortgage lending and LBO transactions are outright Ponzi financing schemes. In both cases, borrowers' cash flow is inadequate to service interest and principal. In subprime mortgages, borrowers are able to increase their borrowings simply from rising collateral value of their houses in the form of home equity loans. Here you get a case of negative amortization, i.e., the principal component of the mortgage increases instead of decreases. In LBOs, a borrower does not have to pay interest from cash flow. It is able to pay in kind, i.e., pay interest using promissory notes issued by another lender in lieu of cash. It can also avoid repayment of principal from cash flow by refinancing or demonstrating rising multiple value. Table 2.1 summarizes the similarities between subprime loans and leveraged buy-out loans.

TABLE 2.1
Similarities Between Subprime and Leveraged Buy-out Loans

Subprime Loans	Leveraged Buy-out Loans
Low equity to loan ratio	High debt/EBIDTA
Interest only payment, negative amortization	Payment in kind
Zero down payment	Lenders provide bridge financing
Cash out refinancing	Cash out through dividend payment
Home price appreciation	Price multiple increasing
Poor credit due diligence	Covenant-lite loans
	You snooze you loose clause

Credit Default Swaps (CDSs)

Another important financial innovation is credit default swap (CDS). Put simply, a CDS is a financial guarantee or insurance provided by a seller (usually a highly rated financial institution) against default by a corporate or sovereign borrower. The buyer of a CDS pays a premium for the guarantee provided by the seller. CDS originated as a hedging instrument and serves the purpose of reducing credit exposure for a lender or investor to a company whose bonds or loans he has purchased. For example, Bank A would like to lend $100 million to Company B, but its credit limit is $50 million. To reduce its credit exposure to Company B, it can either syndicate $50 million of the loan to other banks or purchase a CDS from an issuer, Insurer C, for $50 million. Bank A now takes the credit risk of Insurer C, the CDS issuer, rather than Company B, the original borrower. The putative advantages of CDS are: buyers of CDS are able to hedge their risks, volume of lending in the banking industry can be increased, CDS provides an additional source of market pricing for credit risks (Skeel and Partnoy 2007). On the negative side, they reduce banks' incentive to monitor credit exposure, they are unregulated and opaque, increase systemic risks by bloating the credit system and establishing interconnections between counterparties producing domino-effect from defaults, and provide incentives to holders of CDS to destroy value. This last point is illustrated in the examples of Tower Automotive and AIG and more recently in the restructuring of General Motors where holders of $36 billion of CDS on General Motors are more keen to see the company go bankrupt so that they can collect on the insurance (Sender 2009*a*).

In 2004, as the financial condition of Tower deteriorated, banks that had outstanding loans to the company were willing to restructure the credit. But hedge funds that had bought CDS on Tower had incentive to see it default so they could collect on the guarantees provided by the CDS sellers. Furthermore, some of them shorted the stocks of Tower, standing to gain more from its downfall. In other words, creditors who do not hold the original bonds of a company but who hold CDSs written on that company are less inclined to see a distressed company restructure so that they can collect on the guarantee from the seller of the CDS if the company defaults. The extensive use of CDSs less for protection but more for speculation has created perverse incentives for creditors to see companies go bust rather than restructured, creating more risks for the system. Not only are systemic risks increased with bankruptcies of defaulting borrowers but an overloading of payments by issuers of the CDSs increases the risks of downgrade and defaults by the issuer. This is exactly what happened to AIG that had written too many CDSs and ran into liquidity problems when their credit rating was downgraded.

The problem became worse when speculators shorted AIG's stocks and also bid up the CDSs on AIG's debt so furiously that it accelerated AIG's downward spiral. The price of CDS on AIG reflected that of a bankrupt company when AIG actually had $20 billion in capital infusion from a deal reached with the New York insurance regulators (Gilani 2008*b*). Situations such as this can result in negative basis trading where the CSD spread of a distressed company is higher than its bond spread.

The story of AIG illustrates the pitfalls of CDS (Gilani 2008*a*, 2008*b*, 2008*c*). AIG's basic business of providing insurance is well managed and profitable. What brought the $1 trillion corporation down was the half a trillion dollars worth of CDS written by AIG Financial Products (AIGFP), one of its subsidiaries. AIGFP had sold CDSs with notional value of $447 trillion on esoteric assets like CDOs of subprime mortgages, Alt-A mortgages, and even CDS of CDS. When the bets were in the right direction, AIGFP was making a pile, but when the tides turned, the misplaced bets brought the once mighty empire tumbling down. Being a triple A rated company, AIGFP posted either no or little collateral for the CDSs it issued. However, when the value of these CDOs it insured began to fall, AIGFP had to post more collateral. The problem got worse when AIG's credit rating was downgraded due to the losses suffered. It then had to post even more collateral and soon ran out of cash. The CDSs written were so complex and extensive that even AIGFP did not know the extent of its credit exposure. In early 2008, AIGFP estimated its credit exposure on insuring CDOs was limited to $2.4 billion dollars (Gapper 2008). By mid-September, the hole was estimated at $40 billion. A week later, the Fed had to pour in $85 billion. Another month later the bill rose to $120 billion and at latest count it was $150 billion (Langley et al. 2008; Sorkin and Walsh 2008).

The Federal Reserve Bank was forced to bailout firms like Bear Stearns and AIG because the trillions of dollars of CDSs they had written would be worthless if they failed. All banks and institutions that held these CDSs would not be insured or hedged anymore and would likewise have to suffer losses possibly leading to a meltdown of the entire financial system. AIG was at the centre of this web of interconnected relations. AIG and the Fed initially refused to reveal how the bailout money was used. After much public pressure, it was revealed that a large part of the bailout funds was used to post further collateral to its CDS counterparties. A *Times* article showed the main beneficiaries of the bailout were investment banks and financial institutions. Leading the pack were Goldman Sachs ($12.9 billion), Societe Generale ($11.9 billion), Deutsche Bank ($11.8 billion), Barclays ($8.5 billion) etc. with the top ten counterparties receiving $73 billion (almost half) of the bailout funds pumped into AIG (Saporito 2009, p. 18).

The size of the CDS market rose from virtually zero a decade ago to an estimated $65 trillion in notional value by 2007. What started as a hedging tool became a speculative instrument. It is, as one investment banker said, "taking a view" — taking a view on the credit of a company's or a country's debt. The buyer of a CDS takes a dim view, and the seller a rosy view. If there are not enough underlying bonds or securities to go around, buyers can nevertheless get an exposure to the bonds through the CDS markets. Hence the volume of CDS can be much larger than the volume of underlying securities. Through holding CDS on a company's bond, and through other derivative instruments like shorting, speculators exercise as much influence over a company as its creditors.

The controversies surrounding CDS markets have prompted David Einhorn, one renowned hedge fund investor and player in the CDS market, to call for a ban on CDS. He is quoted as writing, "I think that trying to make safer credit default swaps is like trying to make safer asbestos" (Sender 2009*b*).

Derivatives Market

CDSs and CDOs are only two well-known examples of the derivatives market. When the credit derivatives market started in the late 1990s, there were debates over whether or not they should be regulated. Brooksley Born, the head of Commodity Futures Trading Commission argued for regulation but was opposed by heavy hitters like Alan Greenspan (former Governor of the Fed), Robert Rubin (former Treasury Secretary), and Arthur Levitt (former Chairman of Securities and Exchange Commission (SEC)). In the last days of the Clinton administration, Congress passed the Commodity Futures Modernization Act that exempted derivatives from oversight under state gaming laws, and also excluded certain swaps from being considered as "security" under SEC rules (Dennis and O'Harrow Jr. 2008).

By ruling that credit derivative was neither a security nor a gaming activity, the Act opened the floodgate to derivatives business. Between 2002 and 2007, the notional value of derivatives rose five fold from $100 trillion to $516 trillion — ten times the world GDP (Farrell 2008).

David Roche of Independent Strategy has likened the money and credit system to an inverted pyramid, with narrow and broad money forming 10 per cent of the base, securitized debt the next 10 per cent, and the top 80 per cent consisting of derivatives. Derivative money is not used to purchase material goods but serves to inflate financial asset prices. In long periods of low interest rate environment with low default rates and excess liquidity, the money to be made in the derivatives market is too good to pass over.

This is a period of perfect calm where the "Margins of safety are eroded even as success leads to a belief that the prior — and even the present — margins are too large" (Minsky 1986, p. 220). This was what Savage, the President of AIGFP believed in 1998 when they studied the computer model that predicted that these credit default swaps could be a money spinner with a 99.85 per cent chance of never having to pay out. More recently in an interview he said, "The models suggested that the risk was so remote that the fees were almost free money" (Dennis and O'Harrow Jr. 2008).

Prior to this financial crisis, Greenspan touted the benefits of financial derivatives as though they were God's gift to the financial system. At a 2005 conference at the Federal Reserve Bank of Chicago, he said, "Two years ago at this conference, I argued that the growing array of derivatives and the related application of more sophisticated methods for measuring and managing risks had been key factors underlying the remarkable resilience of the banking system" (Greenspan 2005). On another occasion, he stated, "The history of the development of these [credit derivative] products encourages confidence that many of the new products will be successfully embraced by the markets" (cited in Skeel and Partnoy 2007). Today, his intellectual edifice and his faith in the self-regulatory power of the free market system are shaken though he may not be any humbler.

Derivatives, a large part of the present financial system, unregulated and leveraged to the hilt and embraced by all financial institutions, is a major reason for the fragility and instability of the financial system. Derivatives, which are supposed to derive from and to serve the underlying assets and real transactions, have mutated to become the drivers of the real economy. While there is no doubt, derivatives do and can play a positive role to serve the real economy, they have to be regulated and brought back to saner ground.

The next chapter explains how the financial industry after decades of regulation and relative subordination to the real economy emerged to dominate the U.S. economy again.

Note

1. In April 2002, just before the economic downturn, Greenspan talked about the "dispersion of risk to those willing and able to bear" and how this acts like a shock absorber to prevent "cascading failures" (cited in Wehrfritz 2007; Federal Reserve Board 2002).

3
The Financial Industry Dominates Again

Regulatory Capture[1]

What enabled the financial industry to become so powerful? The financial, insurance and real estate sector (FIRE) has become the largest sector in the U.S. economy. Its share of the U.S. gross domestic product (GDP) rose from 14 per cent in 1960 to 20 per cent in 2006. It is twice as large as the next two sectors — trade at 12 per cent and manufacturing at 11 per cent in 2006. See Figure 3.1. At the same time, the financial industry with its ability to leverage more than non-financial institutions and its financial innovations have earned the industry super profits, and its individual players enormous wealth. Figure 3.2 shows that between 1960 and 2007, the share of total corporate profit earned by the financial sector rose to 30 per cent from 17 per cent while that of the manufacturing sector declined to 21 per cent from 49 per cent. Dealbreaker, a financial blog, calculates that house sales and mortgage securitization generated about $2 trillion in fees between 2003 and 2008 (Gapper 2008). An October 2008 IMF report has raised the estimated losses arising from the financial crisis to $1.4 trillion, up from $980 billion a few months ago (*New York Times*, 7 October 2008).

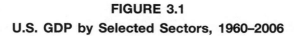

FIGURE 3.1

U.S. GDP by Selected Sectors, 1960–2006

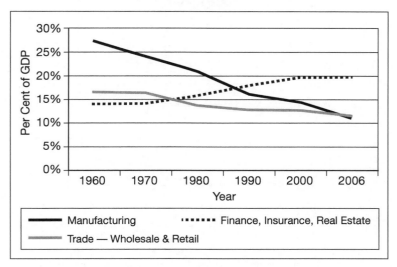

Sources: *Economic Report of the President* (2008), Table B-12.
Economic Report of the President (1997), Table B-10.

At a personal level, Wall Street employees and senior managers have done extremely well. The average compensation on Wall Street was $435,084 per year, ten times that of an average worker in the private sector (Johnston 2007). The chieftains on Wall Street earn over $40 million a year in 2006 and that was over one thousand times the median household income. In 2007, Blankfein, the CEO of Goldman Sachs received compensation of $69 million, and Stanley O'Neal, the former head of Merrill received $161 million upon resignation and after Merrill had made billions of losses in 2007 (Samuelson 2008). The top twenty-five hedge funds managers on average

FIGURE 3.2

Share of U.S. Domestic Corporate Profits by Industry, 1960–2007

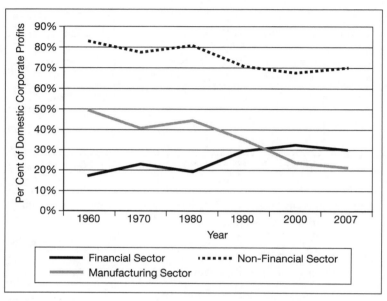

Source: Bureau of Economic Analysis, Tables 6.16A-D.

took home $570 million in 2006 with the top three earning over $1 billion each (Taub 2007).

With such immense wealth and financial power, the financial industry has become the most influential lobbyist in Congress and the White House. Reich, the former Labor Secretary under President Clinton, argues that political democracy in the United States has been hijacked by the corporate rich who pour in billions in donations and employ thousands of highly paid lobbyists on Capitol Hill so that their interest and voice have drown out public interest (Reich 2007). More recently, a California based non-profit organization, Consumer Education Foundation, released a 231-page report detailing how the financial sector had invested more than $5 billion on purchasing political influence in Washington over the past decade. Between 1998 and 2008, it spent $1.7 billion on political contributions, and $3.4 billion on lobbyists numbering over 3,000 who swarm the halls of Congress. Individual firms like Goldman Sachs spent more than $46 million on buying political influence, Citigroup spent $108 million and Merrill Lynch spent $68 million (Litvinsky 2009). These donations were bi-partisan, with 55 per cent going to Republicans and the rest to Democrats, though the balance of power has shifted to the Democrats who took in over half of the 2008 election contributions.

Robert Weissman, the leader of the Report said, "Congress and the Executive Branch responded to legal bribes from the financial sector, rolling back common-sense standards, barring honest regulators from issuing rules to address emerging problems and trashing enforcement efforts" (cited in Litvinsky 2009). Take the case of AIG, one of the largest insurers in the United States with a balance sheet of almost $1 trillion and where its life insurance division alone wrote 81 million life insurance policies with face value of $1.9 trillion. The company successfully lobbied for it to be regulated by the Office of Thrift and Supervision (slated for closure under the Obama plan to revamp regulatory agencies) — a tiny outfit that had only one insurance specialist on its staff (Taibbi 2009). AIG befriended politicians and contributed $9.3 million of campaign money to both Democrats and Republicans between 1990 and 2008, and spent more than $70 million lobbying them over the past decade (Saporito 2009).

In addition to political lobbying, there is a revolving door between Wall Street and Pennsylvania Avenue. Witness the number of Treasury Secretaries who were former CEOs of Wall Street firms, and the many former regulators, central bankers and IMF officials who have moved to senior positions in the financial industry. Regan, Treasury Secretary for President Reagan was former head of Merrill Lynch. Robert Rubin, formerly from Goldman Sachs became President Clinton's Treasury Secretary and then joined as Chairman of Citibank when he left the Clinton administration. Henry Paulson also from Goldman Sachs was Treasury Secretary for President George W. Bush. Stanley Fischer, the former First Deputy Managing Director of International Monetary Fund became President of Citigroup International when he left the IMF. Many of the senior advisors of Clinton, Bush, Obama are major Wall Street players. The Democrats under Clinton came under the orbit of New York finance. Personalities like Robert Rubin, Jon Corzine, Sandy Weill, Roger Altman, Richard Grasso were closely aligned with the Democrats. Today the players included personalities like Rahm Emanuel, the chief of staff of President Obama, who used to work in investment banking; Lawrence Summers, the chief economic advisor to the President Obama who advised D.E. Shaw, a Wall Street firm, and received compensation of $5.2 million over two years (Freeland 2009). Daniel Gross, a Democrat writer, argued, "northeast finance was realigning toward the Democrats" (cited in Phillips 2008, p. 46).

Displacement of Main Street companies by Wall Street firms is evident in the starkly different treatment the Detroit Three received compared to the Wall Street firms in this recent bailout exercise. The former had to go hat-in-hand to beg for $25 billion of soft loans that was turned down the first round, and later forced to appear before Congress a second time to receive only $17 billion, while AIG alone received $150 billion from the Fed and Treasury, and Citibank overnight got a $20 billion cash injection and guarantee support for several hundred billions of its loans (*Straits Times* 2008). It used to be what is good for General Motors is good for the United States; now what is good for AIG or Citibank is good for the United States.

Liberalization and Deregulation

It is accepted today that regulators in the United States failed miserably in their role; they were ideologically and financially intoxicated and fell asleep during their watch over the past few decades. After the Great Depression, the U.S. Government tightened anti-trust laws and banking regulations to protect and stabilize the financial system. One centrepiece legislation was the Glass-Steagall Act that separated commercial from investment banks, and prohibited interstate banking to prevent banks from becoming too big and taking too much risks. The Act also regulated the activities of commercial banks, including interest rates charged and restricted entry into riskier investments.

Economic liberalization and deregulation is the economic counterpart of the Cold War. It gathered momentum

under the Reagan regime and provided fertile ground for
the progressive erosion of regulatory restraining walls.
Reagan came into Washington with his famous seven words
— government is the problem, not the solution. Beginning
in the 1970s, financial institutions lobbied hard to deregulate
the financial industry. Under Reagan, the Garn-St Germain
Act was passed in 1982 that allowed savings and loans
associations to diversify their business into riskier activities
paving the path to their eventual bankruptcies seven years
later. This did not deter commercial banks to lobby hard
for further financial deregulation. Regulatory restrictions
were progressively eroded before for the last vestiges of the
Glass-Steagall Act was scrapped under President Clinton,
and replaced by the Graham-Leach-Bliley Act in 1999.
Commercial banks could now fully engage in all types of
investment banking activities that included not only trading
bonds and other types of securities, but also underwriting
them. The fact that this often created conflicts of interests
did not bother them. For example, there is supposed to be a
Chinese wall separating the commercial lending department
of a bank that provides traditional loans to a company and
the investment banking department of the same bank that
issues and underwrites corporate bonds. While this Chinese
wall may prevent lower-level bank officials from knowing
what the other departments do, this is often not the case
with highly placed bank officials like the Chief Executive
Officer who has access to all information in the bank. Often
banks receive heftier fees for investment banking activities
over commercial loans, hence, the latter are sacrificed (e.g.,
relaxing credit standards for investment banks). The issue
of conflict of interests also applies to financial accounting

firms and more recently rating agencies. Accounting firms were doing both auditing and consulting cum advisory services and the two are sometimes in conflict; the fees derived from consulting and advisory services were more than from auditing with a tendency to relax the latter. In the case of rating agencies, the rating fees were paid not by users but the issuers of securities undermining their credibility.

The decline of lending activities and the rise of investment banking activities in commercial banks can be seen from the data collected by FDIC for all U.S. commercial banks. The ratio of non-interest income (from investment banking) to net interest income (from lending) has risen from 25 per cent to 75 per cent between 1980 and 2005 (Federal Deposit Insurance Corporation 2007, Table CB04). In 1980, net interest income was $56 billion, compared to $14 billion for non-interest income. By 2005, net interest income was $270 billion versus $201 billion for non-interest income. In other words, income from investment banking (fee income and trading income) has risen much faster than income from traditional loans. By nature, investment banking activities are riskier and the profits more volatile than those from commercial banking activities.

Shadow Banking System

Deregulation and liberalization spawned the shadow banking system that is at the heart of this financial crisis. Krugman (2009*a*, pp. 158–64) argues that it is not so much the lack of regulation of the banking industry that caused this crisis; rather it is the total lack of regulation of the shadow banking system that is the root cause. The shadow banking system refers to financial activities and institutions that lie outside the ambit of depository taking institutions. Major players in this system include investment banks, hedge funds, private equity funds, insurance companies, offshore and tax haven financial institutions, money market and mutual funds, off-balance sheet transactions of banks etc. All these are unregulated and even more highly leveraged. The combined balance sheet of the five major investment banks was $4 trillion, compared to that of the top five bank holding companies at $6 trillion (Krugman 2009*a*, p. 161). At its peak, the shadow banking system in the United States held $16 trillion of assets, $4 trillion more than regulated deposit-taking banks (Raja 2009). Regulators trained part of their eyes on banks but allowed the other parts of the financial system to run wild. Because banks are so intimately and intricately tied to the shadow banking system through counterparty, lending and other relationships, when the latter exploded, banks were sucked into the vortex. We saw earlier how risks that were supposed to be distributed by banks to the shadow banking system actually came back via the back door through provision of back-up credit lines to structured investment vehicles. Similarly many banks were exposed to leveraged buy-out loans made to private equity funds through bridge loans that sometimes could not be refinanced. Citibank and many other banks were forced to take back billions of toxic assets from their related SIVs when funding for the latter dried up.

Again, twenty years ago, Minsky's words were prescient, "Hierarchical banking relations can be a source of weakness for the financial system as a whole ... the potential for a domino effect, which can cause a serious disruption, is implicit in a hierarchical financial pattern. The introduction of additional layering of finance, together with the invention of new instruments ... is evidence ... of the increased fragility of the system" (Minsky 1986, pp. 86–87).

Advances in telecommunications and computers have simultaneously globalized and shrunk banking, particularly in foreign exchange trading where billions of dollars are transferred instantaneously across the globe and the market operates worldwide, 24-hours a day. Advances in financial theories, particularly with the advent of pricing options, have pushed trading to higher levels. Trading originally involved only the underlying assets, for example, stocks, bonds, real estate, commodities, etc., but the introduction of derivatives heralded the trading of new securities that were not the underlying assets, but were based on (or derived from) the underlying assets. Such derivative transactions are often highly leveraged. The buyer puts up only a small percentage of capital to buy the option. While the risks to the buyer of the option are limited to the loss of his capital, the risks to the seller of the option are unlimited, unless he is hedged.

There are differing views on the reasons and consequences of financial innovations. Advocates see financial innovations as democratizing credit, making funds available to those who once could not afford it, reducing credit risks by spreading risks to a larger community of investors, increasing efficiencies by merging and taking over companies, and making better use of capital through leverage, as well as better allocation of resources by deploying them to where they can earn higher profits.

Critics view financial innovations as strategies to enhance profits and to run one step ahead of regulations. As early as in the 1950s, Minsky had written about this and postulated that the financial industry undergoes waves of innovation, regulation, deregulation, and periods of stability and instability (Minsky 1957; 1986). Each wave is marked by some new products or techniques, be it junk bonds, LBOs, dotcom and, more recently, subprime loans and CDOs. Human greed is part of nature and as long as the environment and system allow and encourage such behaviour, the consequences are predictable. For example, a major reason for the popularity of SIVs and private equity funds is to avoid disclosure, regulation, monitoring, and taxes. Financial regulators and legislators have woken up to this and at the recent meeting of central bankers in Jackson Hole, European Central Bank chief Trichet, called for tackling unregulated entities that have contributed to the upheaval (Callan et al. 2007). Barney Frank, a United States Senator, said that innovation has outstripped regulation and called for better regulations (Washington 2007).

Economic Value Added (EVA) School

It is often said that bankers and financiers have short memories and tend to repeat their poor lending or trading habits. The issue is not that individual memory of these financiers, but a system that demands profit maximization and where competition and the quest for profit maximization operate quite independent of what an individual thinks or prefers.[2] Bankers and financiers operate in an institution where their individual performance is measured by the profits they bring — nothing else. In the last few decades, the Economic Value Added (EVA) school of thought has provided even greater ideological and theoretical underpinning to this behaviour. It has been wholeheartedly embraced by the captains of industry and finance, and has even spread to the public sector. When the principal author was working in the banking industry, he attended a three-day seminar on EVA organized by the New York Institute of Finance. The instructor, at the start of the seminar, asked participants to list some of the objectives of a business enterprise. The list included things like profit maximization, meeting consumers needs, providing employment, innovation and inventing new products or services, meeting corporate social responsibility, etc. After listing the various objectives on the board, the instructor summed up his point of view, that is, of all these objectives, there is only one that matters, that is, how to maximize shareholders' value; other stakeholders are peripheral. Put simply, EVA states the primary, if not the sole, objective of a company or economic enterprise is to maximize share-holders' value, treating other stakeholders like employees and the public as irrelevant. EVA is the criterion used to measure the performance of every institution, every department, and every individual. EVA is calculated using the net present value of the cash flow of the activity discounted by the weighted average cost of capital. Every activity and individual is compared against this yardstick and the ones with the highest EVA are rewarded. Hence, within the banking system itself, one finds that traditional lending is out of favour as it consumes too much capital and results in lower EVA, whilst activities such as trading in securities and derivatives that use less capital and produce higher EVA are promoted. It then becomes rational for every individual pursing his or her own interest to push to the edge of the envelope, maximize the returns, and worry about the consequences later. A banker who brings in maximum loans is rewarded the same year, but if and when the loans turn bad a few years later, he or she has already moved on. This incentive structure biases the banker to maximize short-term rewards without regard to the long-term risks of their behaviour. There are recent calls for bankers' compensation to be restructured into long-term contracts to take account of eventual risks and failures down the road (Wolf 2008).

It is correct that an investment should have positive, and not negative, net present value, that is, it should be value creating rather than value destroying. However, the larger question is never raised, that is, What is an acceptable level of profits? Should it be maximized at all costs, and at the expense of the public good? Is it the case that what is best for an individual or corporation is always best for the whole economy and society? We return to the issue of the fallacy of composition, that is, what is good for the individual must be good for the whole; the whole is the sum of its parts. This problem is particularly acute for the banking and financial industry because banks are in the unique position to make high rates of returns from their ability to leverage. The ordinary individual or company is limited by its ability to leverage, whereas banks and financial institutions whose business is financial intermediation are able to leverage easily unless they are subjected to regulations. The era of deregulation or light regulation gave the financial institutions a golden opportunity to maximize its profits such that Jim Reid, Head of Credit Research at Deutsche Bank, estimated the U.S. financial sector has made around $1.2 trillion ($1,200 billion) of "excess profits" in the last decade relative to nominal GDP (cited in Foster and Magdoff 2008, p. 11).

Under an economy dominated by the financial sector and the ideology of EVA, the sole criterion by which companies are judged is the maximization of shareholders' value. Consequently, publicly listed companies are focused on short-term gains measured by quarterly profits and stock market valuations rather than long-term development. This puts pressure for management of companies to adopt measures such as corporate downsizing, mergers and acquisitions, leveraged buy-outs etc. to boost profits without considering the long-term effects on the economy. The rampant practice of leveraged buy-out artists to lay off workers, in order to slash costs and boost profits, is a case in point. In the past decades, we have witnessed the phenomenon of jobless growth. Companies are making huge profits and the economy is growing, but jobs are not rising as fast, particularly permanent jobs. What we see is a massive change in the job structure, away from jobs that are more permanent and secure, to contractual, part-time and temporary jobs. All these may be good for corporate profits but they have had disastrous social and economic consequences for the society, one of which is evident today. In the present rebound or nascent "recovery" from this financial crisis, the markets have moved way ahead of the real economy. The U.S. unemployment rate, even though a lag indicator, is at a high of 10 per cent and could be the Achilles heel of the economy. By passing the problems to society at large, we have a classic case of privatization of gains and socialization of costs.

Old Wine in a New Bottle

Applied collectively then, it is not irrational for each individual and each institution to push to the edge of the envelope. What is in the interest for an individual or a bank may, however, not be in the interest of the whole as it creates stresses in the system that results in crisis. This is akin to the prisoners' dilemma wherein rational decisions made by each individual result in collective irrationality. While each player in the financial market may have acted rationally, the aggregate effect has been the build up of systemic risks that eventually blew up the financial system.

Viewed from a historical perspective, the present subprime mortgage crisis is simply a variant of previous crises but with financial innovations that have multiplied risks.[3] It is old wine in new bottle. As a matter of fact, given all the new financial innovations, the underlying cause is not very new. It is no different from the problems of the savings and loans crisis in the 1980s or the Asian financial crisis of the 1990s that resulted from funding mismatches. The Great Depression, the Savings and Loans crisis of the 1980s, the Asian Financial Crisis of mid-1990s, for instance, were the result of similar problems that affected this crisis, i.e., complacency towards risks after long periods of economic stability, moral hazards that caused reckless behaviour among players in financial markets, maturity mismatch between short-term liabilities and long-term assets, currency mismatch between loans and investments, and regulatory failures that did not sufficiently address asset bubbles soon enough or rein in excessive leverage. The difference between past crises and the present one is that the latter has complex financial products with greater leverage that increases manifold the level of financial risks for the system.

The next chapter analyses the structural causes of the crisis and the three macroeconomic imbalances.

Notes

1. This is the term used by Richard Posner (2009*a*) to explain how Wall Street has come to influence the political and regulatory process in the United States.
2. This is illustrated in the *Financial Times*, July 2007 interview with Chuck Prince, the former CEO of Citigroup, who famously said, "When the music stops, in terms of liquidity, things will be complicated. But as long as the music is playing, you've got to get up and dance. We're still dancing."
3. "All financial innovation involves, in one form or another, the creation of debt secured in greater or lesser adequacy by real assets ... All crises have involved debt that, in one fashion or another, has become dangerously out of scale in relation to the underlying means of payment" (John Galbraith, cited in Plender 2009).

4
Structural Changes and Three Macroeconomic Imbalances

The Three Imbalances

Although the immediate causes of the current global financial crisis were due to both market and regulatory failures, the seeds of the crisis were sown decades ago. These can be traced to structural transformation in the economy that led to three major macroeconomic imbalances in the U.S. and the global economy. They are the imbalance between the financial sector and the real economy, the wealth and income imbalance in the distribution of resources in the United States, and the chronic global current account imbalances in the world economy. Put together, these three imbalances provided a fertile environment for the crisis.

Just as an organic or biological system becomes dysfunctional when its components are out of balance, the same happens to an economic and financial system when things are not balanced.

Imbalance Between the Financial and Real Economy

As pointed out in the previous chapter, the financial sector has grown to a point where it has eclipsed the real economy.[1] Between 1960 and 2006, the financial sector (defined as finance, insurance, real estate mortgages and leasing ("FIRE")) rose from 14 per cent to 20 per cent of GDP, while the manufacturing sector more than halved from 27 per cent to 11 per cent of GDP. The big shift occurred circa 1990 when the financial sector overtook the manufacturing sector in terms of GDP contribution. By 2006, not only was FIRE the biggest sector, it was twice as large as the next sector which was wholesale and retail trade at 12.2 per cent. See Figure 3.1.

Post-World War II economic development of the U.S. can be divided into two major periods: the first from mid-1940s to mid-1970s, and the second from mid-1970s to the present. The first thirty years after the war saw rapid growth and also a rise in the real wages and living standards for a majority of the population. This was the Golden Age for the U.S. when it assumed global hegemonic position with the biggest military and economic power and its currency became the international currency. However, after the Vietnam War and the oil shock in the mid-1970s, its rate of growth began to slow down. The average growth rate of real GDP dropped steadily from 4.4 per cent in the 1960s to 3.3 per cent in 1970s and thereafter to 3.1 per cent in the next two decades and further to 2.6 per cent in 2000s. See Figure 4.1.

Debt-Driven Economy

This slow down in growth rate has been associated with, and counteracted by the rise of demand-driven growth through the use of debt and financial asset inflation (Minsky

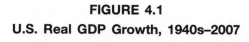

FIGURE 4.1
U.S. Real GDP Growth, 1940s–2007

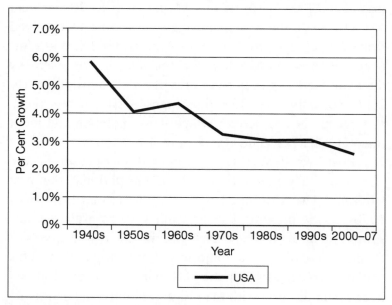

Source: Foster and Magdoff (2008), Table 2.

1986; Foster and Magdoff 2008). Table 4.1, for instance, shows the massive rise in debt in the U.S. economy. Between 1960 and 2007, while GDP rose 27 times (from $526 billion to $14 trillion), total domestic debt grew 64 times ($781 billion to $49.9 trillion).

For many years after World War II until mid-1970s, total U.S. domestic debt as percentage of GDP hovered around 150 per cent. See Figure 4.2. In the following decade it rose to 204 per cent in 1985, and then dramatically escalated after 2000 from 276 per cent to 357 per

TABLE 4.1

U.S. GDP and Domestic Debt by Sectors, 1960–2007

	GDP	Total Debt	Domestic Debt by Sector				Rest of World	Dom Fin + Non-Fin Corp Debt
			Financial Sector	Non-Financial Corp Sector	Household Sector	Government: Local, State, Federal		
	US$ billions	US$ billions	US$ billions	US$ billions	US$ billions	US$ billions	US$ billions	US$ billions
1960	526	781	33	201	216	308	23	234
1965	719	1,107	62	305	339	365	38	367
1970	1,038	1,600	128	514	457	450	52	642
1975	1,638	2,619	260	864	734	663	97	1,124
1980	2,789	4,725	578	1,478	1,396	1,079	193	2,056
1985	4,220	8,623	1,257	2,578	2,278	2,268	243	3,835
1990	5,803	13,769	2,614	3,753	3,598	3,486	318	6,367
1995	7,398	18,475	4,234	4,134	4,857	4,684	567	8,368
2000	9,817	27,143	8,145	6,589	7,011	4,583	815	14,734
2005	12,434	41,244	12,969	8,472	11,740	6,556	1,512	21,441
2007	13,971	49,882	16,155	10,588	13,815	7,313	2,016	26,743
Growth × Time 1960–2007	27	64	490	53	64	24	88	114

Source: *Economic Report of the President* (2008), Table B-1; Federal Reserve Board System, Board of Governors, Flow of Funds Z.1 files, Table L.1 Credit Market Debt Outstanding.

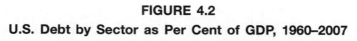

FIGURE 4.2

U.S. Debt by Sector as Per Cent of GDP, 1960–2007

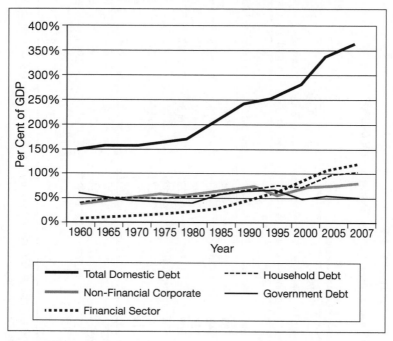

Source: Ibid.

cent in 2007. If the rise in debt is dramatic, the sectoral composition of debt is disconcerting. See Table 4.1. Between 1960 and 2007, the financial sector debt rose an astounding 490 times, while household debt rose 64 times, non-financial corporate debt 53 times and government debt 24 times. No doubt this is due to the fact that financial debt in 1960 started from a tiny base. It was $33 billion at 6 per cent of GDP while the government debt was 59 per cent of GDP.

Table 4.1 also reveals that the level of government debt to GDP is rather stable at between 40 per cent and 60 per cent range, whereas the level of financial sector debt to GDP went from an under-representation of 6 per cent to 116 per cent over the same period. There were two spurts in the growth of financial sector debt: the first after 1980 and the second after 2000 — these coincided with two major financial innovations — the securitization of debt particularly housing mortgages, and the introduction of derivatives such as collateralized debt obligation (CDO) and credit default swap (CDS).

Financial Debt

Figure 4.3 shows in greater detail the composition of the financial sector debt. From 1960–2007, the most significant development was the securitized and real estate related sector (consisting of real estate investment trusts (REITs), asset backed securities, and federal agencies like Fannie Mae, Freddie Mac) became the largest borrowers in the financial debt market. Starting from almost nothing, these accounted for 58 per cent of total financial debt by 2007. Finance companies, on the other hand, have dwindled into insignificance (dropping to 8 per cent from 61 per cent), while commercial bank debt was relatively stable at a range of between 6 per cent and 16 per cent of total financial debt. The estimated value of home mortgages stood at $11 trillion, i.e., 85 per cent of the U.S. GDP in 2007. Some analysts have argued that having housing market prices rise was the Fed's way of compensating for the $7 trillion loss in the stock market

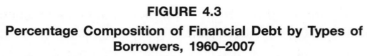

FIGURE 4.3

Percentage Composition of Financial Debt by Types of Borrowers, 1960–2007

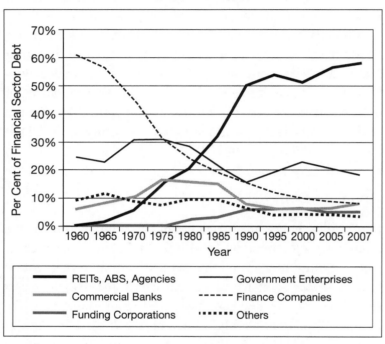

Source: Ibid.

between 2000 and 2002 (Phillips 2008, p. 62). There is no doubt that the Fed in early 2003 dropped interest rate to 1 per cent from over 5 per cent to avoid a bad recession and in the process hastened the housing bubble that finally burst.

In short, the U.S. economy has turned to debt as the main driver of its economy. From a nation of saver with current account surplus, it has become the largest debtor nation in the world with current account deficit reaching more than $800 billion or 6.5 per cent of its 2006 GDP.

Use of Debt

How was the debt used? As capital markets became more sophisticated, the level of investment financing by non-financial corporations switched from internally generated funds to debt. Initially, debt was used for financing fixed investments, but increasingly after 1980s, much of the debt was used for financial leverage. Figure 4.4 shows that even as U.S. corporate debt (financial and non-financial) escalated from under 44 per cent of GDP in 1960 to

FIGURE 4.4

U.S. Corporate Debt vs Corporate Investment, 1960–2007

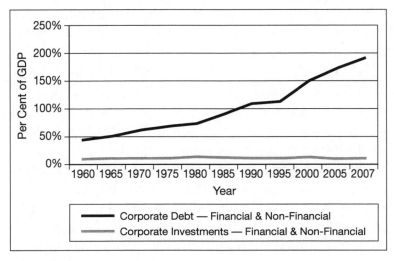

Source: Ibid.

191 per cent in 2007, gross corporate investment as percentage of GDP remained stable at around 10 per cent.

Benjamin Friedman, a Harvard economist, wrote:
"The 1980s has been by far the worst period for business
investment in physical assets like plant and equipment
since World War II. Instead of borrowing to build new
facilities or even to build liquidity, the corporate business
sector as a whole has mostly used the proceeds of its
extraordinary borrowing since 1980 to pay down equity
through mergers and acquisitions, leveraged buy-outs and
stock repurchases ..." (cited in Phillips 2008, p. 40).

The financial sector has grown so huge that instead
of deriving from and serving the underlying transactions
in the real economy it has become the driver of the real
economy. This is happening not only in the U.S. economy
but also globally as the Anglo-Saxon model dictates
the trend in global finance. To illustrate, the volume of
financial assets and transactions has dwarfed the value
of productive investments worldwide. The ratio of global
financial assets to annual world output used to be about
equal (109 per cent) in 1980. By 2005 it was three times
(316 per cent). In terms of value, global financial assets
were $140 trillion (Wolf 2007a). In comparison, the
world's total GDP stood at $48 trillion in 2006 (World
Bank 2007). Another indicator is the foreign exchange
market. Turnover in traditional foreign exchange markets
(spot, forward, and swaps) increased to an unprecedented
level of $3.2 trillion a day, while activity in the over-the-
counter derivatives markets reached $2.1 trillion per day
(BIS 2007); this compared to the volume of world trade
at $12 trillion per year.

The growth of financial innovations had resulted in an explosion of new forms of liquidity, like derivatives, that have truly escalated leverage (Roach D. 2007). The global liquidity market is estimated at $607 trillion or 12.5 times global GDP. See Figure 4.5. Given this scenario, central banks have little control over the global liquidity market and are hard pressed to influence the long-term cost of capital that has been at historic lows. This is sometimes known as the new monetarism. We have arrived at the stage where what happens in the financial markets dictate what happens in the real economy. It is the case of the tail wagging the dog. The booms and busts of the last few decades are caused more by asset price inflation in the financial sector and less by wage and price inflation.

FIGURE 4.5

**Inverted Liquidity Pyramid — Global Liquidity
Market $607 Trillion**

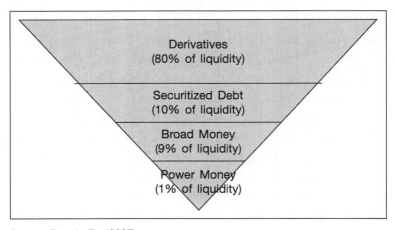

Source: Roach, D. (2007).

The impact of asset price inflation on profits have led Jim Reid, Head of Credit Research at Deutsche Bank to make the following observation: "U.S. financial profits have deviated from the mean over the past decade on a cumulative basis. ... The U.S. financial sector has made around $1.2 trillion ($1,200 billion) of 'excess profits' in the last decade relative to nominal GDP. So mean reversion ... would suggest the $1.2 trillion of profits need to be wiped out before the U.S. financial system can be cleansed of the excesses of the last decade ..." (cited in Foster and Magdoff 2008, p. 11).

Wealth and Income Imbalance — The Neglected Imbalance

A key to understanding the long-term structural cause of the present crisis lies in the relation between economic inequality, debt, and financial innovations and growth. While the U.S economy has been growing, income and wealth distribution has deteriorated after 1970s. The Gini Index for income distribution in the U.S. went from 35 to 46 between 1970–2006 (Burkhauser et al. 2009, p. 18). With a Gini Index of 46.6, U.S. income inequality is closer to the Latin American states like Argentina (52.2) and Mexico (54.6), than to other developed countries like Canada (33.1) and Germany (28.3) (SustainableMiddleClass.com).

Roughly this meant the top 2.7 per cent of households earned one-fifth of all income earned, while the bottom 6 per cent earned only 0.3 per cent (Wikipedia 2009*a*). According to economist Janet Yellen, "the growth (in real income) was heavily concentrated at the very top of the top, that is, the top 1 per cent" (cited in Wikipedia 2009*b*, footnote 34). A recent study by Saez (2008), showed that the share of total income of the top 10 per cent of income earners dropped from 45 per cent (mid-1920s to 1940), to and hovered at 32 per cent (1940s to 1970s), and escalated to 50 per cent by 2006, with the top 1 per cent playing a central role in the evolution of this trend. Between 1993 and 2006, the top 1 per cent income earners captured half of the overall economic growth, with the problem worsening under the Bush administration (2002–06) where they captured three quarters of income growth.

Wealth is even more unevenly distributed in the U.S. with a Gini Index of about 80, i.e., the top 20 per cent owned 85 per cent of total wealth in 2001. More graphically, the top 1 per cent of households owned 33 per cent of total wealth; this is twice the amount of wealth (15 per cent) owned by the bottom 80 per cent. Ownership of financial wealth (that is, excluding house ownership) is even more skewed with the top 1 per cent owning 40 per cent and the bottom 80 per cent only 9 per cent (Domhoff 2006, p. 2).

Among the reasons for this increasing income and wealth inequality are the effects of technology on the job market favouring skill-based professions over blue-collar work, globalization that saw the outsourcing of work overseas, the erosion of union power particularly after Reagan came into power, stagnation of minimum wage, the lag of wage rates behind productivity increases, the huge rise in the compensation of executives following deregulation in the 1980s, and the huge tax breaks given to the rich. Saez (2008) says, "We need to decide as a society whether this increase in income inequality is efficient and acceptable and, if not, what mix of institutional reforms should be developed to counter it."

Figure 4.6 captures some of the above trends. Between 1990 and 2005, while Federal minimum real wage dropped

FIGURE 4.6

Cumulative Percentage Change in Economic Indicators, from 1990 (in 2005 dollars)

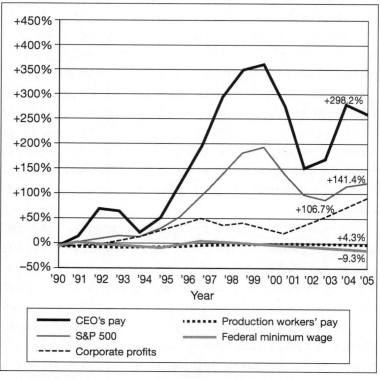

9 per cent and production workers' pay rose 4 per cent, CEOs' average compensation rose to 409 per cent and then dropping to 298 per cent, even though corporate profits only rose 107 per cent.

More significant is the distribution of share of capital income (income from capital gains, dividends, interest and rents) is getting more skewed. Between 1979 and 2003, the share of capital income flowing to the top 1 per cent of households rose from 38 per cent to 58 per cent, while the share going to the bottom 80 per cent halved from 23 per cent to 13 per cent. See Figure 4.7.

FIGURE 4.7
Share of Income by Household Income Category

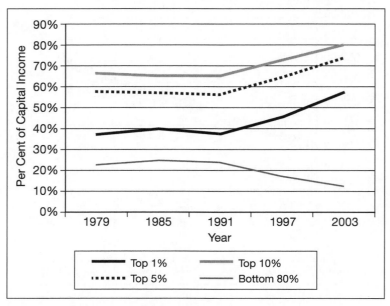

Source: Domhoff, September 2005 (updated May 2009).

For a long time, there was a tight fit between produc-
tivity gains and real wages compensation in the United
States. But this began to diverge radically after the 1970s.
See Figure 4.8. This imbalance worsened drastically under
President Reagan who dismantled the National Relations
Board, broke the back of the air traffic control labour union,
and renegotiated the accord between labour and capital in

FIGURE 4.8

**U.S. Non-Farm Business, Productivity vs Compensation
Per Hour, 1947–2008**

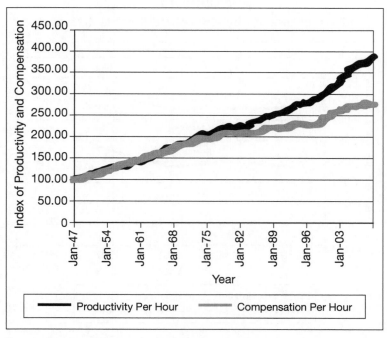

Source: Bureau of Economic Analysis.

favour of the latter (Bowles et al. 1986). Capital's share of income rose with successive tax cuts in dividends, capital gains, corporate earnings, estate duties, and the like. In other words, the share of GDP going to labour versus capital is more a product of political contest and less a result of marginal productivity. Galbraith (2008) likewise argues that inequality is determined less by technology and trade but more by the excesses in profits associated with bubbles in the technology sector in late 1990s, and the other sectors favoured by the Bush administration in the 2000s. These excesses are reflected in stock market appreciation whose benefits are disproportionately enjoyed by a small minority.

Greenspan alluded to this problem in his memoir, but says he is puzzled by it. He admits that profits are much higher than should be in a competitive world and says, "We know in an accounting sense what is causing it" — the share of worker compensation in national income in the United States and other developed countries is unusually low by historical standards — "but we don't know in an economic sense what the processes are". He continues that in the long run, real wages should parallel increases in productivity, but for now it has veered off course for reasons he is not clear about. And he worries that if wages for the average U.S. worker do not start to rise more quickly, political support for free markets may be undermined (cited in Guha 2007). In contrast, Henry Ford, the twentieth century consummate capitalist, understood this conundrum a hundred years ago and called for higher wages for the ordinary workers so that they also could buy the cars produced.

What is the relationship between inequality and the financial crisis? The imbalance in income and wealth impacts the financial sector in contrapuntal ways. Extreme inequality, on the one hand, results in under-consumption for the vast majority of people at the bottom, and on the other hand, excess savings for a tiny minority at the top. Put in another way, the vast majority, with inadequate income and low purchasing power, has a high marginal propensity to consume that could only be met with debt assumption, while a tiny minority with excess savings, and a high marginal propensity to save, has a high appetite for investments.

With the rise of the debt-driven economy, under-consumption for the majority is "solved" through the assumption of debt by the ordinary households. After financial sector debt, household sector debt rose the most — 64 times, from $216 billion to $13.8 trillion between 1960 and 2007. See Table 4.1. At $13.8 trillion, household debt is equivalent to the U.S. GDP. Hence, despite stagnating household incomes, household consumption increased from about 60 per cent of GDP in the 1960s to over 70 per cent in 2007 made possible by more two wage-earners households, people holding multiple jobs, and heavier debt burden. Home equity loans became an important source of "income" for many, and as a driver for economic growth. In 2007, home equity loans totalled $487 billion (*Economic Report of the President* 2008, Table B-72). It was estimated that without home equity withdrawals, U.S. GDP growth would have been negative in 2001 and 2002, and less than 1 per cent between 2003 and 2005 (Wikinvest). This boom, however, ultimately proved to be a bane when house prices began to collapse and the credit crunch spread to all sectors of the economy. Elizabeth Warren, head of a congressional panel to monitor U.S. government bailout plans, realizes that any meaningful address of the financial crisis must start with the repair of the household balance sheet. She said, "Any effective policy has to start with the households. Years of flat wages, low savings and high debt have left America's households extremely vulnerable" (Henriques 2008).

Under-consumption and excess savings are two sides of the same coin. At one end of the spectrum, is a majority without enough income or wealth, and at the other end, is a tiny minority with excess savings and liquidity. As individuals, the rich can only consume so much; most of the income and wealth is invested either personally or through institutions. The raison d'etre of capitalists is not consumption, but investment to beget greater amount of wealth for further investment. This excess savings and liquidity from domestic sources are placed in financial institutions where financial engineers churn out exotic financial instruments to meet the growing demand for higher yields by investors.

Hence economic inequality gives rise to two types of bubbles — a debt bubble assumed by households whose income have stagnated and whose consumption can only be met through taking on more debt; and an asset price bubble that is a consequence of the rich chasing for higher yields, whose risk appetite grows with excessive concentration of wealth. Financial institutions are the main beneficiaries of these bubbles while the going is good. But sooner or later the two bubbles will burst and they did in 2007.

Current Account Imbalance

The final macroeconomic imbalance contributing to the financial crisis that is most talked about by economists is the current account imbalance between trading partners. In particular, the imbalances are between the major current account surplus countries such as emerging Asia, Middle East, Russia and Germany on the one hand, and the United States where deficits are observed every period since early 1980s, except for a brief period in 1991. See Figure 4.9.

FIGURE 4.9

U.S. Current Account Balance and Real Exchange Rate, 1973–2009

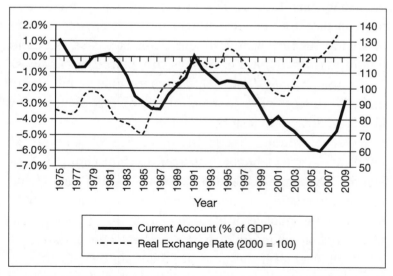

Source: International Financial Statistics (IFS) of the International Monetary Fund.

At its peak in 2006, the U.S. current account deficit reached 6.5 per cent of its GDP. Much of the capital inflows into the United States in recent years financed property related investments and consumption. Figure 4.10 shows the changing composition of debt issuers. After 1996, Federal government debt issue as a percentage of total debt was on the decline for most years, while asset backed securities and debt issued by housing related agencies such as Fannie Mae and Freddie Mac were on the rise.

FIGURE 4.10
U.S. Debt Issuers — Who Issued the Debt?

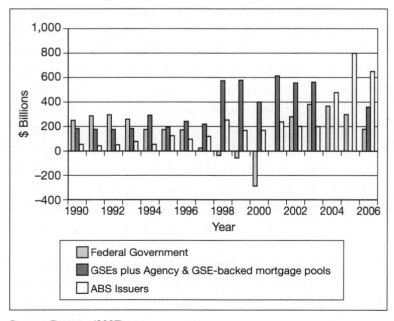

Source: Duncan (2007).

In 1997, the sudden massive outflow of private capital triggered the Asian Financial Crisis (AFC). Since then, most have repaired their economies and have built up large current account surpluses and foreign exchange reserves. Twelve Asian countries hold $4.7 trillion or 56 per cent of the world's foreign reserves. China alone has $2.1 trillion (25 per cent) of the world's reserves (Wikipedia 2009c).

Today, because of huge current account surpluses, emerging Asia and oil producing countries are supporting the consumption habits of the U.S. households and government. In 2006, U.S. public debt (excluding the government's intra-government debt of another $3.8 trillion) stood at $5 trillion, of which 44 per cent was held by foreigners. Foreign central banks with huge reserves owned 64 per cent of this $2.2 trillion. By 2009, China and Japan together held 47 per cent of U.S. foreign debt. China alone held $722 billion in May 2009 (Wikipedia 2009b). According to the report by Hodges (2007), foreign investors accounted for 46 per cent of U.S. Treasury bonds, 27 per cent of corporate bonds, and 14 per cent of government agency bonds. In 2007, the U.S. current account deficit of $790 billion was 93 per cent financed by the combined current account surpluses of China, Japan, Germany, and Saudi Arabia (*Economist* 2007e, p. 98). In other words, ironically, the poorer nations are financing the spending habits of U.S. households, corporations, and the government.

Establishment economists like Greenspan and Bernanke blame the current account surplus countries for causing this imbalance and crisis. Bernanke in his speeches (2005, 2007) is particularly influential and forceful in articulating this view. He argued that the low savings in the United States in the last decade are endogenous to (determined by) external events that contributed to what he called "the global savings glut" in the rest of the world, especially in emerging Asia and the oil producing countries. As a result of excess savings over investment in these countries, abundant global liquidity, available at low interest rates, was responsible for fuelling asset prices and, through their wealth effect on consumption, led to the fall in U.S. savings and to the rise in current account deficit. He attributed the global savings glut to a combination of factors that included, among other things, the desire to amass a "war chest" of foreign reserves by post-AFC emerging Asia to insure against future speculative attacks, pursued using various mechanisms including managed exchange rate systems, and the relative attractiveness of United States as an investment destination for excess global funds. Nothing is said about the many exogenous (determining) events that we have described in the last two chapters that have independently contributed to the U.S. consumption glut. These included the debt-driven culture, the unregulated shadow banking system, the excessive leveraging by the finance and household sectors, and the regulatory failures that allowed the build up of the systemic risks.

Stephen Roach, chairman of Morgan Stanley's Asia operations, was one of the few economists who is deeply critical of the Bernanke view. He wrote (Roach S. 2005):

> There may be a deeper and potentially more sinister meaning behind the saga of the global saving glut. In my view, it is being used as a foil to deflect attention from one of the world's most serious

imbalances — the excess consumption of America's asset-dependent economy ... By focusing on the saving glut, Bernanke conveniently offers a revisionist history and theory that all but exonerates the Fed under Greenspan from any culpability in spawning the world's unprecedented imbalances ... Implicit in the saga of the global saving glut is yet another effort at scapegoating — in effect, pinning the blame on the world's savers while exonerating American consumers and the US central bank from fostering mounting global imbalances. Unfortunately, by failing to face up to its own excesses, the United States does itself and the rest of the world a huge disservice. I've said it from the start: Global rebalancing is an urgent and shared responsibility. The sooner the world seeks a collective resolution of its problems, the less likely a disruptive endgame.

Note

1. This section on structural changes in the U.S. economy owes much to the seminal works of Palley (2007), Phillips (2008), and Foster and Magdoff (2008).

5
Impact on Asia and Challenges Ahead

The global financial crisis that began at the epicentre spread forcefully across the globe and affected nearly every economy, big or small. We now look at the impact on and challenges to Asia.

The Asian Financial Crisis of 1997 ("AFC")

Not long after Asia recovered from the Asian Financial Crisis (AFC), it is hit with another crisis in 2007; this time the epicentre was the United States. While each crisis is different from another, they share enough common characteristics from which valuable lessons can be drawn.

It is generally accepted that what happened in Asia before the AFC was the influx of foreign capital that resulted in misallocation of capital, mismatch of short-term borrowings with long-term investments, aggravated by pegged exchange rates. In the early 1990s, interest rates in developed countries were low and investors were chasing for higher yields in the "emerging markets" starting in Latin America and culminating in Southeast Asia. In 1990 private capital flows in emerging markets were $42 billion and by 1997, they reached $256 billion (Krugman 2009a, p. 79). Most of these were short-term capital flows in the form of portfolio investments and other investments (loans and deposits) through the banking system.

Faced with huge capital inflows, it is almost inevitable that much went into speculative investments in the stock and property markets, or ended up in financially unviable projects. From the experience of one of the authors as a debt restructuring specialist in Southeast Asia during the AFC, it was commonly known among financial specialists that in the heyday of bank syndicated loans, both foreign and local banks were lending more than what was required or financially viable. Like the subprime saga of today, lenders and borrowers had over-optimistic financial projections at best, or engaged in fraud and financial mismanagement at worst. The results were asset bubbles and over-leveraged corporations with foreign currency loans that imploded when sudden massive reversal of capital flows caused huge depreciation in the borrowers' currencies (Corden 2007).

The AFC was not the boom and bust of a normal business cycle but one associated with speculative and erratic financial flows. The current account deficits in many countries before the AFC were not the result of low savings rates. In fact, savings rates remained steady and high by global standards; the negative savings-investment gaps widened as a result of rising private investments funded by an abundance of cheap foreign private capital. In 1996, five Asian countries, South Korea, Indonesia, Malaysia, Thailand and the Philippines, received net private capital inflows of $93 billion; a year later they experienced an outflow of $12 billion, a turnaround of $105 billion, amounting to more than 10 per cent of their combined GDP (Rodrik 1998). No country can sustain this magnitude of financial reversal without a crisis. In a matter of months the financial contagion spread throughout Asia and brought many economies to their knees. Real GDP in 1998 fell by 13 per cent in Indonesia, 11 per cent in Thailand, 7 per cent in South Korea, 7 per cent in Malaysia, 5 per cent in Hong Kong, 1 per cent in Japan and 0.8 per cent in Singapore (Lee and McKibbin 2007). It is instructive to note that two countries that did not fully open up their economies to capital flows — India and China — were spared the ravages of the AFC.

What lessons did the Asian countries learn from the AFC and what did they do? Governments had little choice but to bailout the financial systems through takeover of bad banks, wide scale restructuring of bad loans with government participation, and reforms in the financial sector and legal systems. The fiscal costs of bailouts in these countries, as a percentage of GDP, ranged from a high of 55 per cent in Indonesia to 13 per cent in the Philippines. See Table 5.1.

TABLE 5.1

Costs of Banking Crisis during Asian Financial Crisis

Countries	Fiscal Cost (% of GDP)	Output Loss (% of GDP)	Non-Performing Loans at Peak (% of Total Loans)
Indonesia	55	39	70
Malaysia	16	33	30
Philippines	13	10	20
Thailand	35	40	33

Source: Caprio et al. (2003).

Table 5.2 shows that these countries have since cleaned up their non-performing loans, introduced legal and banking reforms, improved financial regulation and supervision, and strengthened capital adequacy ratios. One important lesson learned was for corporations to reduce leverage and to minimize currency mismatch of their debt. Between 1996/97 and 2006/07, corporate balance sheets of these countries became healthier with corporate debt to equity ratios declining significantly: from 41 per cent to 13 per cent for the Philippines, and 119 per cent to 46 per cent for Indonesia. Also, a favourable global economic environment, after the 2000 dotcom crisis, boosted exports and Asian economies rebounded in terms of output levels, but the growth rates of real output is still lower than the pre-crisis levels (Khor and Kit 2008, pp. 85–87). Table 5.3 shows healthy improvement in macroeconomic indicators for five ASEAN countries between 1997 and 2007. Current account balances turned from deficits to surpluses, foreign reserves rose dramatically, external debt ratio improved, and fiscal deficits are low.

The debate is not settled whether policy-makers in Asian countries adopted mercantilist policies and managed their foreign exchange rates to build up reserves to protect themselves against possible future speculative currency attacks, or the current account surpluses were "forced" upon them by circumstance. What is clear, however, is the remarkable accumulation of foreign reserves by Asian countries, particularly China, that today account for close to 60 per cent of the world's total foreign reserves and this stood the countries in good stead.

TABLE 5.2

Selected Financial Indicators for ASEAN-5

Per Cent	Non-Performing Loans/Total Loans		Risk Weighted Capital Adequacy		Loan to Deposit		Debt/Equity	
	1999	2007/08	1999	2007/08	1996/97	2006/07	1996/97	2006/07
Indonesia	33	9	7	21	105	63	119	46
Malaysia	17	7	13	13	96	71	49	32
Philippines	15	6	18	16	99	59	41	13
Singapore	5	2	21	14	111	74	48	28
Thailand	39	8	12	15	136	91	117	39

Sources: ADB (2008), Table 3; MAS (2008).

TABLE 5.3

Selected Economic Indicators for ASEAN-5 in Percentage of GDP

	Current Account Balance		Foreign Reserves (US$ Bn)		External Debt		Fiscal Balance	
	1997	2007	1997	2007	1996/97	2006/07	1996/97	2006/07
Indonesia	−2.3%	2.4%	16.6	55.0	51.0%	33.0%	0.0%	−1.0%
Malaysia	−5.9%	15.5%	20.8	101.0	40.0%	32.0%	2.0%	−3.0%
Philippines	−5.3%	4.9%	7.3	30.2	49.0%	42.0%	0.0%	−1.0%
Singapore	15.6%	23.4%	71.4	163.0	NA	NA	0.0%	−1.0%
Thailand	−8.1%	5.7%	26.2	85.0	66.0%	27.0%	3.0%	1.0%

Sources: MAS (2008), Table C-1; IFS (various issues).

Impact of Present Crisis on Asia

Despite healthier macroeconomic fundamentals and minimal exposure of domestic Asian banks to toxic assets related to the U.S. subprime market, emerging Asian economies were hit hard by the current financial crisis because of their closer integration into global finance and trade.

At the peak of the current global financial crisis, credit spread hikes were observed during the last quarter of 2008. Stock markets in Asia declined more compared to those in G2 countries. Between the end of 2007 and beginning of 2009, while the Dow Jones index and UK FTSE fell by 34.1 per cent and 30.2 per cent respectively, Japan Nikkei fell by 42 per cent, Shanghai Composite by 64.3 per cent, and Korea KOSPI by 36.4 per cent. Asian stock markets fell as foreign funds withdrew to cover for losses suffered in the United States. In the same period Asian currencies depreciated but not as sharply as during the AFC. Except for the yen and the reminbi that appreciated by 18.7 per cent and 6.6 per cent respectively, others like the Korean won depreciated by 34.9 per cent, the Indian rupee by 23.7 per cent, the Thai baht by 3.5 per cent, and the Taiwan dollar by 1.3 per cent. The Korean won was hit hardest because of its disproportionate exposure to foreign portfolio investments; Korea's external debt swelled to $425.1 billion in the second quarter of 2008 and its loan-to-deposit ratio of 140 per cent in the banking sector outstripped other countries in the region (Pio 2009). Depreciation of the won would have been worse if not for government bailout that was possible during this crisis because of its sizeable foreign reserves built up after the AFC.

In the real economy, Asia saw the greatest collapse of its export markets due to a sharp decline in imports of goods and services by the developed economies. The main reasons were the credit crunch that affected investments and trade, and the negative wealth effect on consumption from losses suffered in the financial meltdown. In January 2009, large decline in exports were observed, ranging from 40 per cent year-on-year for Taiwan and the Philippines, around 35 per cent for Indonesia, Singapore and Korea, and circa 25 per cent for Malaysia, Thailand and Hong Kong. Only China registered a less than 20 per cent decline in exports (World Bank 2009, p. 13). The collapse is broad based ranging from industrial equipment, electronics, and commodities to garments that make up a large part of Asia's exports. Other exports such as tourism also suffered with Thailand as the biggest victim, its problem compounded by domestic political tension.

In terms of GDP contraction, while the U.S. and Europe declined at an average of 5 per cent in fourth quarter 2008 and first quarter 2009, countries most open to trade and finance suffered even more acute decline, many of them in Asia. By global standards, Hong Kong and Singapore are the most open followed by, Korea, Taiwan, Thailand, and Malaysia and they experienced declines, in annualized rates, ranging from 13 per cent to 20 per cent points. Growth fell somewhat less severely in the Philippines and only moderately in Australia and New Zealand. Real GDP growth remained positive throughout the crisis in Indonesia, China, India, and Indonesia, but even those fast-growing economies experienced noticeable declines in growth relative to earlier trends. In Europe, the sharpest decline occurred in Germany, with the most open economy to trade (Bernanke 2009).

Policy Responses

The policy responses to the crisis called for coordinated action among members of the global economy to use aggressive monetary and fiscal policies to compensate for the collapse of private sector demand.[1] Obviously, countries that have stronger macroeconomic fundamentals have greater scope to pursue more aggressive monetary and fiscal policies. In terms of monetary policies, those that have lower inflation rates such as China, Japan and Thailand were able to pursue a more expansionary monetary policy without the fear of raising inflation; whereas Indonesia, the Philippines and Korea are more muted in monetary response because of inflationary concerns. As for fiscal stimulus, China put up the biggest package equivalent to 12 per cent of its GDP, followed by Malaysia 9 per cent, Singapore 8 per cent, Korea 7 per cent, all exceeding U.S. stimulus package as a percentage of GDP (World Bank 2009).

The Asian response to the crisis appears to be working. Table 5.4 shows that in the second quarter of 2009, although exports have partially recovered relative to pre-crisis peaks, industrial production has outperformed exports except for New Zealand and Hong Kong. In fact, industrial production in China, India and Indonesia has exceeded pre-crisis levels, and is within 5 per cent of the pre-crisis level for Australia and Korea. The revival of domestic demand in Asia has, in turn, aided global economic growth.

Table 5.4

**Asian Industrial Production and Exports Relative
to Pre-Crisis Peaks (2009 Q2)**

Country	Industrial Production	Exports
China	1.07	0.73
India	1.04	0.70
Indonesia	1.00	0.74
Australia	0.96	0.68
Korea	0.94	0.76
Thailand	0.89	0.73
Singapore	0.88	0.69
New Zealand	0.88	0.90
Malaysia	0.87	0.67
Hong Kong	0.85	0.88
Philippines	0.82	0.71
Taiwan	0.81	0.77
Japan	0.71	0.64

Source: CEIC, Haver and Staff Estimates (cited in Bernanke 2009).

Indeed the strong performance in Asian recovery has quickened the pace of global recovery. A recent IMF report predicted that while the global economy will contract 1 per cent in 2009 and grow at 3 per cent in 2010 (IMF 2009c, p. xiv), emerging Asia will grow at 5 per cent and 6.8 per cent, with China growing at 8.5 per cent, India 5.4 per cent and Indonesia at 4 per cent in 2009 (Ibid, pp. 73–74). Other indicators are also doing well for Asia;

stock markets and housing markets have recovered strongly over the last six months, especially in China, Hong Kong and Singapore; inflation is negligible and unemployment is much milder than past recessions.

Is this remarkable recovery of Asia an indication that it has decoupled from G2? There is insufficient evidence at this point to reach a positive conclusion. Asia's sharp fall was clearly due to the contraction in global trade. Its recovery is due to a return towards normalcy in credit and trade. This strong recovery would not have been possible without healthy corporate balance sheets and macroeconomic fundamentals that were put in place as a result of the pain experienced during the AFC.

The jury is still out as to whether the recovery would have the inertia to sustain itself once the fiscal stimulus is taken away. This would depend critically on the speed and strength of economic recovery in the G2 and when the fiscal stimulus can be retracted.

What is Next?

The big challenge is where will Asia go from here over the medium and long term? The export-led growth model has served Asian countries well over the last few decades, starting with Japan, followed by the Asian tigers and now China. All these countries exported their way to prosperity. Starting from a low economic base with non-existent domestic markets, these countries grew by depending on foreign investments and foreign markets for the goods produced. In the early stages, most of these countries experienced current account deficits; capital goods were imported to build up an industrial base producing goods for the export markets. Over time, through investments and production, they built up formidable export sectors, and deficits turned into surpluses with periods of ups and downs following the global business cycles. In the last few years, following the aftermath of the AFC, Asian countries, led by China, entered a long period of export boom and enjoyed recurrent surpluses.

The success of the Asian export story generated a new set of contradictions in the form of global current account imbalances between Asia and the United States. As trade imbalances are nothing more than a reflection of savings-investment gaps between trading nations, it is important to understand why investments are higher than savings in some countries resulting in current account deficits, and why investments are lower than savings in other countries leading to current account surpluses?

For Asian economies such as Malaysia, Thailand and South Korea, the bursting of asset bubbles during the AFC left behind excess capacity and the need to repair their balance sheet. Consequently, investment levels dropped and have not recovered to their previous levels. This is the main reason why savings, which have remained stable, exceeded investments. This led to increasing current account surpluses and, together with a managed exchange rate, contributed to a build up of substantial amounts of official foreign reserves.

For countries like China that was hardly affected by the AFC, the current account surpluses rose exponentially over most of this decade due to a combination of factors. Growth in productivity in labour intensive manufacturing and managed exchange rate contributed to attractive pricing of Chinese exports. This combined with a high savings rate led to current account surpluses. In 2006 for instance, China's total savings from government, household and the corporate sectors was 50 per cent of GDP, of which the bulk was by the corporate sector (28 per cent), and the household sector (15 per cent). The household sector saved for precautionary reasons. For instance, even the poor are forced to save because of deterioration in access to health care, education and social security. A serious illness and visit to a hospital could cost an ordinary worker up to two years of his annual wages. Similarly he/she has to save because of insufficiency of state-provided subsidies for social security and educational services. The corporate sector, on the other hand, saved much because of low wages paid to workers, and the absence of taxes and dividends paid to government. The net result was a large current account surplus. This plus intervention in the foreign exchange market led to an accumulation of foreign reserves of over \$2 trillion (Corden 2009).

For the United States, its current account deficit (see Figure 4.9) rose from near zero per cent of GDP in 1991 to a peak of 6.5 per cent in 2006, with most of the increase occurring after the dotcom bust in 2001. Whereas its deficits from 1991 to 2000 were driven mainly by a rise in private investment and consumption connected with the dotcom investment boom, the accelerating deficits from 2001 to 2007 were driven mostly by budget deficits and rising consumption connected with housing market boom.

It should be noted that while the abundance of foreign liquidity at low interest may have fanned the housing bubble, it has also brought benefits to the U.S. economy. First, low interest rate enables countries in need of capital to finance their investments cheaply. Second, the U.S. Treasury and its citizens have benefitted from low interest rate loans from abroad. Third, its consumers, particularly workers whose real wages have lagged behind productivity for many years, enjoy cheap products from China.

It is also interesting to note that although the U.S. and China have approximately the same Gini coefficients in the mid-1940s, they exhibit different savings and consumption behaviour. High income inequality in China resulted in high household savings rate, while the U.S. household sector ended up with low or even negative savings rate. This anomaly can be explained by the divergence in consumer credit facilities and culture between the two countries. In China, the consumer credit markets are under-developed, whereas in the U.S., all kinds of consumer credit are available including borrowing to consume against rising asset prices.

The more fundamental concern over current account imbalances is not the low interest rate environment but rather the huge international debt accumulated by the United States from several decades of current account deficits. Is this debt sustainable? If not, what steps should been taken to solve this problem before it causes another international financial crisis? Besides the necessary adjustments in exchange rates, the United States clearly need to save more and spend less; this mean exporting more and importing less from the rest of the world.

Since the peak of global economic crisis in 2008, the U.S. current account deficit has narrowed to about 3 per cent of GDP in 2009. This decline has come about despite a ballooning budget deficit of about 10 per cent of GDP for 2009. This means that private savings-investment gap must be chalking a positive 7 per cent of GDP. The corporate sector's investment has been affected by the liquidity crunch, and the household sector, badly over-stretched, are repairing their balance sheet and starting to save. Personal savings rate, at zero per cent in April 2008 has surged to 6.9 per cent in May 2009 (Miller and Sider 2009).

Is this readjustment in savings a temporary blip or is it a longer-term trend? In either case, it is clear that the United States cannot go on accumulating international debt at the present rate without triggering another international financial crisis. It has to narrow its chronic current deficit by either increasing its gross savings or reducing its gross investment. How will Asia respond and readjust?

Three Challenges for Asia

Limits of Export-Led Growth Model

There are two alternatives for Asia. The first is for Asia to continue on its export-driven growth and find other con-sumer(s) of last resort and who will that be? The second is to increase domestic investments and consumption. As to the first option, it is unlikely that Europe or Japan can assume that role. That leaves the Asian domestic markets as the alternative. However this is limited by the increasing income and wealth inequality that we have raised earlier unless there is a major restructuring of its economies.

The Chinese Government, for instance, now recognizes that the supercharged growth it pursued over the last two decades is unbalanced, unstable and unsustainable. China's growth was powered by high levels of exports and investments that together account for about 80 per cent of its GDP growth (Roach S. 2009, p. 173). Consumption as a percentage of GDP dropped from 55 per cent in 1970 to 36 per cent in 2006 (Roach S. 2009, p. 240). Between 1998 and 2005, the World Bank estimated the share of GDP accruing to labour declined from 53 per cent to 41 per cent (*Economist* 2007*f*); whereas the average for the developed economies is about 65 per cent. Seen from another angle, the wage increases of Chinese workers have fallen behind productivity gains in the country. Productivity growth in Chinese industry averaged 20 per cent per annum compared to wage increases of 12 per cent between 2000 and 2004 (Roach S. 2009, p. 186).

If China wants to decrease savings and increase consumption as a driver of economic growth, it has to reduce income inequality on top of improving social services and social safety net for the majority of the population. Wage increases should keep up with productivity increases and the imbalance between the share of GDP going to capital versus labour has to be addressed. Countries such as South Korea and Taiwan, for instance, have seen significant drop in inequality as their economies grew. It is necessary for China to do the same to maintain social stability and cohesion.

In looking to domestic consumption as an alternative to exports to stimulate growth, Asian countries should not follow the Anglo-Saxon model of pumping up domestic consumption through debt creation. Mohamad Nor Yakub, the Second Minister for Finance of Malaysia, in a recent interview with CNBC said he would like to see consumption in Malaysia increase from 51 per cent of GDP to 70 per cent. This ratio will put it on par with the U.S. consumption level as a proportion of its GDP. We have identified that one of the structural causes of the financial crisis is the increasing imbalance in wealth and income distribution contributing to increase in household debt as a way to sustain a high level of consumption. Malaysia's Gini coefficient is at 49, higher than that in the United States. The country's total bank loans are skewed to private consumption with 55 per cent directed to households in the form of residential and non-residential property loans (36 per cent), passenger car loans (10 per cent), credit cards and personal loans (7 per cent). Sixty per cent of its households earn US$900 per month. Without increasing household income or improving its income and wealth distribution profile, pumping up consumption through debt creation could take it down the same path as the United States. In fact, this is a policy challenge for most Asian countries, particularly China, that are attempting to turn to the domestic consumption as an engine of growth.

What about increasing domestic investments to reduce current account surplus? In the case of China, investments are at high levels of 45 per cent to 50 per cent but much of these are directed at production of goods for export and at physical infrastructures. The issue is not so much increasing the level of investments but rebalancing the mix or composition of investments to reap greater social returns. If some of the corporate savings can be taxed by the government and redirected to social infrastructure such as education, health care and social security, this would help to correct a number of problems: first, investment in health care and social security services would reduce the need for excessive precautionary savings that in turn would increase household consumption and improve the general welfare of the present generation. Furthermore, it would also help to narrow its current account surplus. Second, improved knowledge and skills through educational services would contribute to long run growth as knowledge and skills are key drivers of productivity. Finally, education improves social mobility and contributes to reducing income inequality.

The above is not a call for autarchy and an abandonment of export-led growth but a recognition of its limits, and a rebalancing towards domestic growth and regional integration especially for countries that do not have large domestic markets. Particularly for countries with huge foreign reserve surplus, instead of investing these savings in and financing deficits in the West, they should invest more within the region to raise growth, income and consumption within the region and reduce dependence on G2 regions (Ariff 2009). To achieve this, Asian countries must redouble their efforts at regional integration at various levels — coordination of foreign exchange rate mechanisms, monetary cooperation, and regional investments — and learn to forgo some sovereignty for common benefit. A strengthened Asia should continue to be outward looking and be engaged with the rest of the world.

Relooking at Capital Flows

Two of the most important aspects of globalization today are free capital flows and floating exchange rates, with many countries practising intermediate foreign exchange regimes. While capital flows freely, labour is not allowed to move freely globally; this asymmetry is a cause of financial imbalances and instability (Koo 2008, pp. 205–08).

The demise of the fixed exchange rate regime under the Bretton Woods system in the 1970s ushered in the period of floating exchange rates and also quickened the pace of capital flows. Beginning in the early 1970s, the United States started to liberalize capital flows by removing restrictions on capital account transactions. This recipe was aggressively promoted by Washington and the IMF and adopted by other developed and developing countries. The U.S. financial institutions stood to gain most from the internationalization of finance — free floating exchange rates and free capital flows. This is clearly evident in the change in the composition of banks' revenue. Banks began to derive more and more profits from trading, particularly trading of currencies, and less from their traditional lending activities. This trend was accelerated by technological changes and financial innovations. Billions of dollars could now be transferred electronically and instantaneously; exchange rates of currencies changed by the minute; interest rate and currency options and other forms of derivatives were invented and traded. "Between 1972 and 1985, the size of the international banking market increased at a compound annual growth rate of 21.4 per cent." (Ubiq Consultancy 2009).

Capital Flows and Financial Crises

Theoretically, exchange rate movements are determined by two forces — purchasing power parity (PPP) and interest rate parity (IRP). The former refers to trade flows and the latter to capital flows. If there is no capital flow, exchange rate movements would be driven mainly by PPP forces. This means that a country with current account deficit (or surplus) would eventually have such deficit (surplus) corrected through price adjustment via the depreciation (appreciation) of its exchange rate at some point in time. However, with the introduction of free capital flows, exchange rates can and do move in opposite direction from trade flows. For example in the early 1980s, the United States ran large fiscal deficits that led to persistent current account deficits. This should, according to PPP forces, weaken the U.S. dollar. But because interest rates were higher in the United States, capital flowed in, the dollar appreciated, U.S. trade competitiveness weakened and its current account deficit worsened (see Figure 4.9). This eventually led to a currency crisis that had to be corrected through the Plaza Accord in 1985 where coordinated foreign exchange intervention by the G5 averted precipitous fall in the U.S. dollar. This temporary solution was followed with a more permanent one through the Lourve Accord in 1987 wherein the United States agreed to reduce its fiscal and deficits while Japan and Germany agreed to do the opposite.

We have earlier discussed how capital flows and their sudden reversals have been responsible for triggering the AFC and will not repeat it.

Carry Trades and Crises

Besides the AFC, there are other financial crises that are intimately connected with short-term private capital flows. Examples are the "carry trades" where one borrows from a country with low interest rates and invests in another with higher interest rates. The profit is the spread between the two interest rates but the risk is the appreciation of the borrowed currency. The yen carry trade refers to borrowings from Japan, a country that traditionally has low interest rates. In the present crisis, the Fed responded with aggressive monetary policy reducing interest rates to near zero. As a result, we now observe a rise of dollar carry trade where one borrows in U.S. dollar to invest in assets of higher yielding currencies.

While no one knows exactly the volume of carry trades worldwide, estimates run to the tune of trillions of dollars. The first wave of yen carry trades started in the late 1980s when financial speculators borrowed in yen and invested in European securities. This ended in 1993 after the collapse of the Japanese stock and property markets and Japanese investors retreated home and the yen appreciated. The second round began in the summer of 1995 and ended in late 1998 after Russia defaulted, Long Term Capital Management collapsed, and the Japanese Government started to recapitalize its domestic banks.

Over the past several years, carry traders inflated several emerging stock markets to astronomical heights, and also boosted more mature stock markets in the developed economies. But the unwinding of carry trades is a destructive force not only to global stock markets but also currency markets. From August to mid-October 2008, as yen carry trades unwound, the yen surged against the Brazilian real, the Australian dollar, the New Zealand kiwi, the British pound, and the Euro — all high yielding currencies that were the traditional targets of yen carry trades (Dorsch 2008).

Currency speculation in the form of carry trades undermines national monetary policies and aggravates current account imbalances particularly of smaller economies (Koo 2008, pp. 197–205). For example, with interest rates pegged at 7.25 per cent since December 2005, the highest among industrialized countries, New Zealand was one of several countries that became a hot target for hedge funds borrowing low-interest yen. This contributed to the country's asset bubble causing the Reserve Bank of New Zealand to cool its domestic economy by raising interest rates. That ended up attracting even greater inflow of capital that further appreciated its currency and worsened its current account deficit to nearly 9.5 per cent of its GDP, and its net foreign liabilities to 80 per cent of its GDP (Kwok 2007). The country was buffeted by adverse shifts in foreign investment sentiments; finally the Reserve Bank intervened in the currency markets to push down the Kiwi dollar while raising domestic interest rates to cool the economy.

Today, short-term capital flows dominate over trade and direct investment flows. This is nowhere more evident than in the volume of foreign exchange trades versus the volume of world trade. In 2007, the volume of world trade was in the region of $12 trillion dollars, while the volume of foreign exchange trades (both plain spot and forward trades plus the derivative trades) amounted to $5 trillion a day or $1,300 trillion per working year — a multiple of 260 times. Granted the volume of foreign exchange transactions is a notional value and could include some double counting, nevertheless, it is a clear indication that financial speculation is a large part of currency trades and has severe destabilizing effects on real economies.

Pros and Cons of Free Capital Flows

The debate over capital controls is not new (Forbes 2008). As far back as 1920s, Ragnar Nurkse wrote about "destabilizing capital flows"; and in the 1970s, Charles Kindleberger described the role of capital in driving markets into "manias, panics and crashes". In fact, immediately after World War II, Keynes and other delegates, architects of the Bretton Woods' fixed exchange rate system, debated over the role of capital controls and eventually adopted free capital movement for current account transactions but allowed countries to exercise discretion over controls for financial account transactions.

Over the following years, controls were lifted, first by developed countries in the 1970s and later, by developing economies. Free capital flows appeared to have raised investments, growth and asset prices. However, sentiments over capital liberalization started to wane after a series of financial crises ravaged emerging economies, starting with Asia in 1997. Malaysia took the bold step to impose capital controls on capital outflow to prevent a precipitous fall in currency values that had happened to other neighbouring countries such as Indonesia, Korea and Thailand.

The IMF initially opposed the measures but subsequently and reluctantly accepted the validity of these capital control measures after it received heavy criticisms from many prominent economists for the way it handled the AFC. Thereafter, many leading policy-makers and economists began to support capital controls especially in developing economies where financial institutions and governance are not yet fully developed. From 2002 to 2005, Colombia, Russia and Venezuela implemented new controls on capital inflows to dampen appreciation of their currencies. Over the same period, however, some large emerging markets (e.g. India and China) moved in the opposite direction and liberalized existing controls.

There are benefits and costs to free movement of capital. The benefits are financing for investments and growth; long-term direct investments, for instance, bring in not only capital but also technology and international market networks. Capital outflows allow domestic citizens and companies to earn higher returns and better diversify risks. On the other hand, free movement of capital causes extreme volatility in exchange rates; rapid capital inflows and outflows can ravage small economies and complicate a country's ability to pursue independent monetary policies. Finally, massive and sudden capital inflows misallocate capital leading frequently to over-investments and creating asset bubbles that ultimately crash.

Whether controls are desirable should be determined empirically. Several empirical macroeconomic studies on how capital liberalization impacts economic growth show mixed results (see Prasad et al. 2003). The reasons are: problems of aggregation make it difficult to distinguish between different types of controls, the types of capital flows, and differences in institutional ability to implement controls (Eichengreen 2003; Forbes 2008; Magud and Reinhart 2006; Prasad et al. 2003).

On the other hand, microeconomic studies, see for example Forbes (2006), argue that controls raise the cost of capital especially for smaller firms; reduce market discipline in financial markets leading to inefficient allocation of resources; distort decision making by firms and individuals as they attempt to evade or minimize the costs of controls; and controls are difficult and costly to implement even in countries with sound institutions and low level of corruption.

The microeconomic studies are useful in highlighting how different sources of inefficiency can arise from controls; but they have overlooked or underestimated that controls may have positive effects such as reducing or removing inefficiences arising from other sources like imperfect information, bounded rationality or incomplete markets. Rodrik (1998) and Bhagwati (1998*b*), for instance, argue that free capital flows are not the same thing as free trade. Capital flows are prone to market failures arising from asymmetric information, incompleteness of contingent markets, and bounded rationality. As a result, they can move in ways that are not predictable, especially with short-term capital flows. Stiglitz (1998) calls for more transparency of capital movements but this is difficult to do especially with private capital flows. Most economists agree that while developed economies with strong financial institutions should have few capital controls, developing economies with weak financial systems and underdeveloped financial institutions are highly vulnerable to financial crisis with free capital flow. Tobin (1978) proposed "throwing sand in the wheels" of short-run capital flows by imposing a uniform tax on all foreign exchange transactions. This would discourage short-term capital flows, but with negligible effects on long-term flows. Others (such as Akyuz 2009) suggested imposing prudential rules like capital and liquidity requirements, in a counter-cyclical manner, on financial institutions to reduce currency mismatches, maturity mismatches, as well as mismatches undertaken by the corporate customers of financial institutions.

Bhagwati (1998*b*) suggests that countries like India and China, that still have not completely shed their controls on capital, should not do so until they have attained political stability, sustained prosperity and substantial macroeconomic expertise. These countries should perhaps gradually lift their capital controls as they grow and develop, but there is disagreement on the sequencing and timing of these reforms.

Asia's Reserves and Alternative International Currencies?

The U.S. dollar has been the dominant international currency for the greater part of the last century. However, Avinash Persaud wrote in (2004):

> ... reserve currencies come and go. They don't last forever. International currencies in the past have included the Chinese Liang and Greek drachma, coined in the fifth century B.C., the silver punch-marked coins of fourth century India, the Roman

denari, the Byzantine solidus and Islamic dinar of the middle-ages, the Venetian ducato of the Renaissance, the seventeenth century Dutch guilder and of course, more recently, sterling and the dollar.

The United Kingdom lost its dominant position to the United States as the world's largest economy in 1872 and as the world's largest exporter in 1915. The switch from net debtor to net creditor position for the United States started after World War I as the U.S. dollar emerged as a convertible net creditor currency, and became widely used in finance and trade. By 1945, the pound was replaced as the dominant international currency (Chinn and Frankel 2008). Today, the United States is a net debtor similar to Britain's status after World War I, and China is the world's largest creditor. In purchasing power parity terms, Maddison (2007) predicts that China's GDP will surpass that of the United States by 2015. If history is any guide, it is likely that the U.S. dollar could lose its dominant international currency position by the middle of this century. The big question is what will replace it? Will that position be assumed by another country, and who is that likely candidate? Or will it be a world of multipolar international currencies? Or will it be an international currency that is not tied to one country and its national interest but rather an international arrangement akin to the Special Drawing Rights (SDR) that was introduced in Bretton Woods but never really took off?

An international currency plays two important roles — as a medium of exchange and a store of value, in addition to being a unit of accounting. As a medium of exchange, the U.S. dollar is still the predominant international currency. About 50 per cent of world trade are transacted in U.S. dollar, 20 per cent are in Euro and the rest in other currencies. Oil, the world's most traded commodity, is transacted in U.S. dollar. This was accepted by the Gulf states in return for the United States' military protection; much in the same manner when Europe and Japan accepted the U.S. dollar as the international currency under the Bretton Woods system. The Euro is a relatively new currency. While it has made important progress, it is still a distant second and poses no challenge to the U.S. dollar. While countries in the neighbourhood of the Eurozone transact mostly in Euro, the U.S. dollar is still the main currency for transactions in Asia. Given the growing financial clout of China on the world stage and its vast foreign reserves and trading connections, this financial crisis has provided China with the impetus to promote alternatives. This includes the recent experiments of China to use the reminbi as the trading currency for transactions with Russia, some Asian and even Latin American countries. China has also allowed institutions in Hong Kong to issue bonds denominated in reminbi, a first step in creating a deeper market for its currency. This is merely a first step and it has a long way to go.

As a store of value, portfolio diversification by foreign reserves holders is necessary to minimize the risk of dollar depreciation. This is a real concern for countries like China that hold large amounts of foreign reserves. The Euro has provided a substitute to the dollar as a reserve currency, although the dollar still dominates by a ratio of two to one due to reasons such as network externalities and the depth of the U.S. debt market. It is possible in the not too distant future for the reminbi to be a contender but that would depend on the speed at which China can reform its financial markets so that countries that hold reminbi would find it convenient to use it both for transactions purposes and as a store of value.

In March 2009, China's Central Bank Governor, called for a super-sovereign currency, like the SDR, to replace the current system based on sovereign currencies. This idea is gaining momentum as it was also mooted by Russia, and proposed by the Stiglitz Commission under the aegis of the U.N. General Assembly (United Nations 2009).

The rationale for this proposal is that the current international monetary system has two fundamental flaws; it is both unstable and inequitable.

It is unstable because conflict may arise whenever a national currency is used as an international reserve currency. Just as one instrument may not be able to achieve two targets that are sometimes in conflict, the use of a sovereign's currency as an international currency may result in a conflict between meeting national goals of full employment and growth and the international goal of providing an optimal level of international liquidity.

Under the Bretton Woods agreement of fixed exchange rates, the U.S. dollar became the global reserve currency together with gold under the condition that convertibility is guaranteed at $35 per oz. of gold. Immediately after World War II, both gold and dollars were scarce for the rest of the world, and the demand for dollars for trade and as official foreign reserves was made possible by the United States running balance of payments deficits. This suited the United States too as it was running fiscal and balance of payment deficits to meet its national objectives of domestic full employment and of maintaining global economic and military hegemony. This arrangement worked well in the beginning when the U.S. dollar was scarce for the rest of the world but became a problem in late 1960s when the accumulated dollars held as reserves outside the United States far exceeded the amount of gold held by the United States. Many countries (especially France) wanted the United States to tighten its domestic policies and reverse its balance of payment deficit, but this would reduce the growth of international liquidity and risk a global recession. This catch-22 situation was first enunciated by Robert Triffin (1961) and is now famously known as the Triffin paradox. The U.S. administration was not receptive to the French proposal as this was contrary to its national objectives (Kregel 1999). The result was a continuation of U.S. balance of payments deficits and accumulation of more dollar reserves by foreign central banks. This eventually led to a crisis in 1971 when President Nixon removed the convertibility of dollar to gold at the agreed price of $35 per oz.; an action that effectively destroyed the Bretton Woods fixed exchange rate system.

Moving to a flexible exchange rate system did not remove the basic paradox or inherent conflict in using a national currency as an international reserve currency. The chronic account deficit of the U.S. economy over the last three decades (see Table 4.9) together with the excessive amount of dollar reserves held by export surplus nations are once again threatening the stability of the U.S. dollar whose depreciation would erode the value of dollar reserves held by the rest of the world. But if the United States were to reverse its deficits by saving more and spending less in order to stabilize the dollar, it risks a deepening of its domestic economic recession that may eventually lead to another global recession, unless it can significantly increase its exports.

Besides being unstable, the current international monetary system is also inequitable. The United States as the issuer of the international currency, effectively enjoys interest-free loans from the rest of the world. This is a transfer of resources from the rest of the world holding dollars as a reserve currency. To the extent that poorer developing countries are holding most of the reserves, this is reverse aid from the poor to the rich.

In sum, while the dollar has served the global economy well as a dominant reserve currency since World War II, it is also a constant source of global instability and inequity. They are the two main reasons behind the recent calls by China and the Stiglitz Commission (United Nations 2009) to use an alternative currency, the SDR, to replace the dollar as the international currency.

The proposal to use an international currency, such as the SDR, not pegged to a particular sovereign state is one way of restoring global stability and equity. However, there remain many challenges (Ocampo 2009) and the road map for this proposal is still uncertain.

Note

1. According to a recent IMF report, the world has pumped in $12 trillion of stimulus programmes to jump start the world economy (Gilbert 2009).

6
The Three Contested Terrains

We now return to higher grounds, to locate the financial crisis in a larger historical context. The financial crisis should be seen in the context of contests for hegemony in three areas: a contest for continued political and economic dominance in the international monetary system by the United States; a contest for the continued dominance of the financial industry over the real economy; and finally a contest for continuation of intellectual dominance by neo-liberals and market fundamentalists.

Contest for Continuation of U.S. International Monetary Dominance

We have shown the links between the international monetary system and the financial crisis: how current account imbalances are associated with excess savings in some countries and over consumption in others; how capital flows have trumped trade flows after the collapse of the Bretton Woods system leading to exchange rate instability and undermining the independence of monetary policies.

In particular we have argued that the problem of current account imbalances globally has less to do with countries that have current account surpluses and more to do with a country that is able to defy the "normal rules" of the international monetary system. Under the present international monetary system, it is not possible for most countries to register persistent current account deficits, particularly of a large magnitude, over a long period. Sooner or later market forces will force a correction in their current account deficits and the countries have to live within their means. The United States, however, has been able to defy this trend for a long period. Except for a brief period in 1991, it has registered current account deficits since 1985 rising to a peak of 6.5 per cent of its GDP in 2006. This is because the United States issues dollar that is used as the major international currency not only for transactions but also as a store of value.

An issuer of international currency enjoys important privileges (Cohen 2009, p. 3). The first is seigniorage, in simple language, the ability to print money to pay back your liabilities. All central banks have the power of seigniorage. As the dominant international currency, seigniorage confers the ability to the United States to pay back its dollar obligations in U.S. dollar. In effect, it can borrow and repay without limits as long as other countries want to hold the U.S. dollar. The second privilege is the macroeconomic flexibility to finance external deficits with its own money that is held as reserves by the creditor nations. This amount can be very large. Today, more than two thirds of the world's $8.5 trillion foreign reserves are held in U.S. dollar.

Emerging weak after the Second World War and faced with the rise of the Soviet Union, the rest of the non-communist world was willing to accept a subordinate position in the international monetary system in return for military protection from the United States. This was also the case with most of the Gulf states who accepted the U.S. dollar as the currency of exchange in the oil market.

The United States makes no pretense of its intention to continue holding to its monetary dominance in the world (Cohen 2009, p. 3). The international monetary system is dominated by the United States, and the IMF is the institution that implements the policies of this system. It acts as the lender of last resort to countries that experience dollar liquidity crisis. The IMF rescue packages come with stringent, one-size-fits-all, conditions that have proved disastrous in the AFC. After that crisis broke out in mid-1997, Asian countries, led by Japan, tried to set up an Asian Monetary Fund, as an alternative to the IMF rescue fund. While such a proposal did not present any threat or challenge to the hegemony of the United States and the IMF, the United States probably did not want to allow a precedent to be started where regional cooperation or blocs could assert some degree of independence. Both the United States and IMF opposed the idea and the Asian Monetary Fund never saw the light of the day (Masaki 2007; IMF 2006a). Asian countries a few years later floated a modified and watered down scheme, known as the Chiang Mai Initiative, in which $80 billion of bilateral swap lines were set up for countries with dollar liquidity problems. However, even these facilities were subjected to IMF conditionalities.[1]

The emergence of China and other countries such as Russia, Brazil and India (BRIC countries) with about $3 trillion of foreign reserves has reignited interest and efforts to search for alternatives. China ahead of the G-20 summit in April 2009, called for the greater use of SDR, based on a basket of currencies like the dollar, yen, sterling and euro, as a non-sovereign reserve currency and also for the expansion of the basket to include other currencies like the reminbi. Under this scheme, countries with dollars could exchange dollars for SDRs. The other BRIC countries back China's proposal. On another front, China is promoting the use of reminbi as a trading currency. From 6 July 2009 onwards, selected firms in five Chinese cities can use the renminbi to settle transactions with businesses in Hong Kong, Macau and ASEAN countries. China also agreed to use their currencies in bilateral trade with Russia. Similar arrangements are discussed with Brazil (*Economist* 2009d).

With the demise of the Cold War, one of the pillars for U.S. dominance in the international monetary order in terms of the security umbrella offered is no longer important (Galbraith 2008, p. 202ff). While it may still have some bite for countries like Japan and the Gulf states, it certainly does not figure much for the BRIC countries. It is unlikely there will emerge an alternative single currency to challenge the U.S. dollar. More likely is the emergence of several co-anchor currencies that will dilute the hegemony of the U.S. dollar as a trading and reserve currency. Meanwhile that road will be long and bumpy.

Contest for Dominance by the Financial Industry

We have demonstrated how the financial industry in the United States has grown to become the largest in terms of contribution to GDP, taking in a disproportionate amount of total corporate profits. Because the financial industry is perceived as too important to fail, and too interconnected to collapse, this has encouraged the industry to engage in moral hazard behaviour, laying off externalities for society to bear.

Since the end of the nineteenth century, the financial industry has passed through three major eras in the United States (Krugman 2009*b*): the first phase — the golden or baronial age of finance lasted till the Great Depression of 1929; the second phase lasted about fifty years from the 1930s to late 1970s when banks became regulated and banking became boring; the third phase started from 1980s onwards when banks and other financial institutions became increasingly deregulated and captured not only the U.S. economy but also political and regulatory institutions.

Golden Age of Finance Prior to 1930s

In the era prior to the 1930s, the banking industry was closely connected to and supported industrialization and the advent of major industries.[2] Banks and corporations were closely interlocked. Banks supplied the capital to nascent and important industries such as railroads, telephone and telegraph, shipping, canal construction, steel, minerals and chemicals industries. Banks were the major intermediaries between the providers and users of capital. This golden age was best exemplified by the legendary banker JP Morgan who acquired not only immense wealth but power and influence in economic, political and cultural spheres.

JP Morgan moved in the circles of presidents, princes and even popes.[3]

This period of industrial development was accompanied by a great wave of mergers and acquisitions. The House of Morgan was closely associated with the railroad industry that, like many other industries, over expanded, ran aground and had to be reorganized by bankers. In fact, J.P. Morgan's stamp on restructuring and reorganizing the railroad industry was so pervasive that the process was termed "morganization" (Chernow 1990, p. 67). Bankers also introduced trust companies where stockholders of constituent companies would trade their shares in these companies for "trust certificates" or shares in the trust companies, which are the equivalent of the modern holding companies. The economic and financial power of Wall Street bankers multiplied through these trust companies that grew like wild mushrooms after a spring rain. In 1928, 186 investment trusts were organized. By early 1929, they were being promoted at approximately one each business day. One company that came late into this investment trust business was Goldman Sachs. But that did not prevent its entry from being flamboyant. It sponsored the Goldman Sachs Trading Corporation that launched two major investment trusts — the Shenandoah Corporation and the Blue Ridge Corporation. In a period of less than one month in 1929, Goldman Sachs issued more than a quarter billion dollars of securities that would have invited the envy of the U.S. Treasury. These trusts were unregulated and highly leveraged; their activities pumped up the stock market to such heights that it eventually crashed in 1929. By 1932, in a U.S. Senate Hearing,

Mr Sachs sheepishly replying to Senator Couzens said the stock price of Goldman Sachs Trading Corporation was worth about $1, from its initial offering price of $104 (Galbraith 1997, pp. 49–65).

This period of "robber-baron" finance, to quote Chernow (1990, p. 68), was accompanied by two features that are found in today's financial industry, namely, an explosion of debt, especially household debt, and a ballooning of rewards to financiers. Household debt during the period between World War I and 1929 almost doubled as a percentage of the U.S. GDP. The remuneration of bankers and financiers during this golden age period of finance was much higher than their counterparts in the non-financial industries (Krugman 2009*b*; Philippon and Reshef 2009).

Regulated Finance — 1930s to 1970s

With the Great Crash, the U.S. economy entered into its worst depression with thousands of banks failing, businesses going bankrupt, production plummeting and unemployment soaring into unseen territory. Everyone from Presidents Hoover and Roosevelt to the ordinary folks viewed banks and financial institutions as the main culprits of the mess. After many congressional hearings, the famous Glass-Steagall Act was passed in 1933 that separated commercial banking from investment banking. This Act took aim at the House of Morgan that had combined the two forms of banking to make spectacular profits. It used customers' deposits for speculative investments, dragging down both.

Chernow, writing in 1990 on the rationale behind the Glass-Steagall Act, reveals how little we have learned from the Great Depression and leaves us with an eerie sense of *déjà vu.*

> Foremost, it [the Glass-Steagall Act] was meant to restore a certain amount of sobriety to American finance. In the 1920s, the banker had gone from a person of sober rectitude to a huckster who encouraged people to gamble on risky stocks and bonds. ... It was also argued that the union of deposits and securities banking created potential conflicts of interest. Banks could take bad loans, repackage them as bonds, and fob them off on investors, as National City had done with Latin American loans. They could even lend investors the money to buy the bonds. A final problem with the banks' brokerage affiliates was that they forced the Federal Reserve System to stand behind both depositors and speculators. (Chernow 1990, p. 375)

With the passage of this Act and other acts like the Securities Act, banking and finance entered into an era of strong government regulation. Banking became more sober and boring; bankers were more conservative in lending. Cross-border lending and international banking went into cold storage for over two decades until the Bretton Woods system restored confidence in international finance and trade (Moffitt 1983, p. 42).

This period of regulation also coincided with a fall in debt levels; especially household debt as a percentage of GDP fell sharply during the Depression years and World War II and they stayed below the pre-1930s level for a while. Banking also became far less lucrative. According

to Philippon and Reshef (2009), the wages in the financial
sector declined during this period and was more in line
with that in the non-financial sector. Significantly, this era
of boring banking was also an era of spectacular economic
progress for most Americans (Krugman 2009*b*).

Financiers: Masters of the Universe Again — 1980s to the Present

All these were to change. Finance emerged from relative
hibernation beginning in the 1970s with the U.S. and
world economy going through a series of crises on the
one hand — the collapse of the Bretton Woods system,
U.S. burgeoning and persistent deficits, decline of the
U.S. dollar, oil shocks and finally stagflation; and the re-
emergence of international finance following on the heels
of the U.S. multinational corporations expanding abroad,
on the other hand. The stage was further bolstered with
the ideology of deregulation under Reagan.

We have earlier discussed global financial instability
and how it contributed to the spurt in trading activities
and income of banks. The other trend was the boom in
U.S. multinational corporate activities abroad and the
boost it gave to international lending. Banks had to keep
pace with the multinationals that were operating abroad
and whose profits from abroad determined their well
being. Banks not only had to serve the financing needs
of these corporations but also to "hedge" and protect their
profits. In a volatile international financial system where
interest rates and exchange rates move constantly, poor
money management can wipe out your gains. "The more

money you make overseas, the more money you may be losing", warns New York's Chemical Bank (Moffitt 1983, pp. 43–44).

International banking really took off in the 1970s. Back in the 1950s, only about three major U.S. banks had foreign branches. In 1965, only $9 billion, or 2 per cent of U.S. total banking loans were overseas loans; by 1976, loans of U.S. foreign branches rose 20 times to $219 billion where domestic loans had merely tripled. Domestic inflation, severe recession of 1974–75, and large real estate losses reduced domestic earnings of U.S. banks. They were saved by profits from foreign activities. A basic transformation had occurred — the ten largest U.S. banks made about half of their profits from abroad (Moffitt 1983, pp. 50–51).

This was also the era of financial innovations that we have described earlier. The mergers and acquisition mania, the reintroduction of junk bonds, a market that had been dead since the Great Depression, and the explosion of management leveraged buy-out provided the grit to produce spectacular episodes (takeover of Nabisco) and personalities (Michael Miliken and Ivan Borsky) that were chronicled in books and movies.[4]

All these could not have been possible without the shift in political winds, and the push towards deregulation particularly in the financial industry. Slowly banks became exciting again, corporate and household debt began to rise eventually reaching the pre-1930 levels. By 2000, financial industry at 20 per cent of GDP became twice as large as the next sector (trade) but took in 33 per cent of total domestic corporate profits. Remunerations in the financial industry once again took off after 1990s and left wages in the other sectors far behind. See Figure 6.1. Philippon and Reshef (2009), estimate that rents accounted for 30 per cent to 50 per cent of the wage differential between the financial sector and the rest of the private sector, and that this differential is not sustainable in the long run.[5] The recent spate of bonuses paid to bankers just after banks and other financial institutions have been rescued with government funds attests to the continued powers of the financial industry. Given the regulatory capture that Posner wrote about, it is an unequal contest between the public who have borne the major costs of the crisis and the financial industry that has privatized most of the gains.

FIGURE 6.1

Historical Excess Wage in the Financial Sector

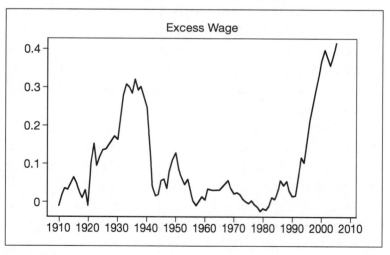

Source: Philippon and Reshef (2009).

Contest of Ideas — Neo-liberals and Market Fundamentalists versus Keynes-Minsky

Great ideas, ideology and theories do not arise in social vacuum; they are usually born in times of crises, and as a reaction against the dominant ideas of the day that have been called into question by the crises. Theories, ideas, including science, must be located and understood in historical context; they are subjected to the same processes of contestations, in this case the contest for intellectual hegemony. The magnitude and severity of today's financial crisis is significant enough to challenge the ideological/intellectual hegemony of neo-liberalism and market fundamentalism that has held sway since the 1970s.

The ideas and economic policies of Keynes and neo-Keynesians were dominant after the Great Depression and the Second World War. Even though Britain was politically and economically weak, Keynes' ideas were seminal to the establishment of the post-war international monetary architecture. Some have argued that it was not even the New Deal that pulled the world out of the Great Depression and that it was the Second World War and the reconstruction after the war that did the trick. Contrary to popular belief, history shows that the state played pivotal roles in almost all major spurts in economic development such as in the rise of capitalism, the recovery after the Great Depression, and the reconstruction after the Second World War (Martinez 2009, chapters 3, 6).

Yet by the late 1970s, beset with a multitude of economic problems ranging from high inflation and unemployment, to deficits and high interest rates, neo-Keynesian macroeconomic policies seemed unable to cure the problems. Several strands of economic thinking came together to contest Keynesianism. These were best represented by the work of Friedman who argued that while the Keynesian model may be relevant in the short run it is not applicable over the long run. This idea was taken to the extreme first by Lucas (1977) and then by Kydland and Prescott (1982) who argued that Keynesian model is not relevant even in the short run. Building on Friedman's idea of efficient markets, they postulated the real business cycle (RBC) model based on the assumption that the market always clears. They showed that business cycles, or booms and busts in the economy, can occur but only because of shocks on the supply side and not on the demand side.

This theory implies there is no room for government intervention to mitigate booms and busts using either monetary or fiscal policies to affect aggregate demand. The RBC theory has been criticized by neo-Keynesians such as Summers (1986) who argued most of the recessions that are observed are driven by demand shocks rather than by supply shocks. Notwithstanding the criticisms, Lucas, Kydland and Prescott were given Nobel prize for their contributions to macroeconomic theory, and the spirit of their work continues to influence the general belief in the efficiency of markets and that government intervention only makes things worse. Friedman in his introduction to the German language version of Hayek's book, *The Road to Serfdom*, argued against the rising "collectivist" tide and cited the increase in U.S.

government spending as an emerging socialist threat to individual freedom. His solution is to "roll back the collectivist state which became one of the hallmarks of his life's work" (Martinez 2009, p. 6). The influence on efficient market theory on the public is best illustrated by President Reagan's famous words when he came to Washington that government is part of the problem, not the solution.

The "efficient market hypothesis" idea had enormous impact on policy-makers, central bankers and people in the field of finance. They believed that the market can do no wrong. For politicians and policy-makers, deregulation and the taming of labour were the tools to fight stag-flation. Deregulation that started under President Carter was taken to new heights under President Reagan who applied it with messianic zeal to the financial sector that eventually led to the bubble and collapse of the savings and loans associations. The neo-liberals also regarded labour "rigidity" as contributing to stagflation, and under Reagan they effectively broke the back of labour and brought down real wages. From thereon, income inequality started to rise uninterruptedly and reached pre-1930s level. Market efficiency is about enlargement of the economic pie and not about distribution; the latter is achieved, if at all, through the trickle-down effect. This belief is taken to its extremes by supply-side economists who had considerable influence over Reagan's and George W. Bush's policies that reduced taxes for the rich ostensibly to spur economic growth. This redistribution of income to the rich accounts for the serious deterioration of income and wealth inequality in the United States.

As described earlier, the re-emergence of finance in the U.S. economy is correlated to and blessed by this line of economic thinking. With the political ground made fertile through deregulation, market efficiency theories inspired a wave of financial innovations that they claimed would do wonders for the economy. They received theoretical legitimacy from the likes of Robert Merton and Myron Scholes who were awarded the Nobel prize in economics for their work in this field. But as it turns out the market was not so efficient after all. The Long Term Capital Management, a hedge fund, based on their rational-market ideas blew up in 1998. Still their theories held sway until it took a bigger crisis, like the present one, to shock Greenspan into admission that "the whole intellectual edifice collapsed" (*Economist* 2009c, p. 83). More recently, Paul Krugman, another Nobel laureate, in his Lionel Robbins Memorial Lectures (2009c) at the London School of Economics took stock of the contributions of mainstream macroeconomic theory over the past thirty years and concluded that they were "useless at best and harmful at worst".

Significantly, the rhetoric of the market fundamentalists was not matched by their practices, or more accurately, their rhetoric was selectively applied. This was apparent in the Federal Reserve Bank's policy bias against consumer price inflation but not asset price inflation. Even more flagrant was the central bank's non-interventionist policy when asset prices are on the rise but clearly interventionist when asset prices have burst. Market fundamentalists are zealous in the fight against labour rigidities but clearly accommodating to the rents enjoyed by the financial industry.

Krugman in the same lecture referred to the works of Keynes and Minsky and said they have been burnished by the crisis. We have earlier referred to this alternative paradigm in explaining the crisis. Instead of assuming financial markets tend towards equilibrium, markets are inherently unstable, lurching from one state to another, driven less by individual rational decisions and more by uncertainty, speculation, herd mentality, greed, and fear. This instability is further exacerbated by positive rather than negative feedback processes that accentuate rather than correct market forces (Soros 2003).

According to Keynes, investments are inherently unstable because decisions are made in a world of uncertainty, and expectations of future profits (marginal efficiency of capital) are essentially incalculable. Investments are made not only on the basis of probable forecasts ("objective") but also on the confidence ("subjective") with which the forecasts are made. This discrepancy between "objective" and "subjective", or speculative profit expectations, explains the violent swings from booms to busts. In periods of booms or overconfidence, the subjective prevails over the objective. This will eventually lead to excesses ensuring a bust, a period of over-pessimism (Burkett and Wohar 1987). Minsky's brilliant contribution was to show that risks build up during periods of overconfidence rather than periods of pessimism. In other words stability breeds instability. Another significant contribution is the role he ascribes to the financial system in causing financial crisis that spills into the real economy. We now know financial markets, instead of being sideshows in economic crises, are the main sources for economic crises of major proportions.

What Lies Ahead

Will neo-liberalism and market fundamentalism be still dominant? Will fundamental reforms be carried out? Can another bigger crisis be averted?

Richard Posner in reviewing the Obama Administration's report on Financial Regulatory Reform (2009*b*) wrote that the report is premature in two respects. First, it advocates a prescription or treatment for a sickness whose causes have not been adequately understood or determined. As he says, "But in the case of the current economic crisis, unless the causes are understood, it will be impossible to come up with good solutions" (Posner 2009*b*). Second, the proposals are not consistent and well thought through.

In an interview with *Xinhua* on 26 June 2009, Joseph Stiglitz, a Nobel laureate who chaired the UN Commission of Experts on the Reforms of International Monetary and Financial System, commented that the Obama report (Department of Treasury 2009) goes in the right direction but is not enough. He said, "There were some good things. For example, the creation of a financial product safety commission, providing consumer protection, is something that I've strongly supported" (*People's Daily Online* 2009). He has, however, various misgivings. "The sad part was that there is no proposal to effectively deal with the too-big-to-fail banks. We need to break them up and we need to restrict the kind of lending activities, risk taking activities that the very large banks can undertake." Under the Obama proposal, much of which will be subjected to approval by Congress, the government will make the Fed a systemic risk regulator to oversee large institutions whose failure could threaten the stability of the entire system. Hedge funds, derivatives and consumer mortgages, will be all under the supervision of the government. To that Stiglitz remarked: "... The problem is the Federal Reserve did not do the job that it was supposed to do. The Fed was in large measure, responsible for the problems that the country is in and the world is in ...". He further added: "The difficulty or the worry is ... that the U.S. Treasury is too connected to the financial markets ... and they reflect the interests of the financial markets, not the interests of the American people" (*People's Daily Online* 2009).

We have in this book tried to identify the causes of the present crisis at various levels — from the theoretical, to the industry practices or malpractices, to the pitfalls in the international monetary system. Beyond the short-term monetary and fiscal responses carried by practically all countries, will meaningful reforms be made both in the national and international financial systems to address these causes? Is there enough intellectual thinking to challenge the neo-liberal, market fundamentalist mode of thought? Is the public adequately informed of the causes and consequences of the crisis? Is there enough sentiment to stop the financial industry from continuing to hold the public hostage to its excesses? Are policy-makers tinkering with the financial system or making meaningful reforms? Will the financial industry continue to have the same degree of political clout? Are Asian countries that have followed the Anglo-Saxon models of finance, the conventional models of export growth, and the accumulation of vast foreign reserves, rethinking new ways of achieving a kind of growth that is more sustainable and balanced

— economically and ecologically? Are we willing to learn the lessons of this great crisis? Or shall these come to pass for naught?

These are the challenges facing us.

Notes

1. With this present crisis, the Chiang Mai Initiative fund has been expanded to $120 billion and converted to multilateral swap lines.

2. This is well captured in Chernow's book *The House of Morgan* (1990).

3. After an audience with Pope Pius X in 1905, the Pope remarked, "What a pity I did not think of asking Mr. Morgan to give us some advice about our finances." *The House of Morgan* would later provide financial advice to the papacy on purchases of American stocks (Chernow 1990, p. 79).

4. The sleuth of books that were published included *Barbarians at the Gate*, *Predators' Ball*, *Pokers' Liar* and the famous film *Wall Street*.

5. After controlling for education, skills intensity and employment risks, wages in the financial industry are consistently higher than those in the non-financial sector, attributable to rent and unobservable factors. The degree of "excess wage" varies between the three periods. Figure 6.1 shows two peak periods of excess wage, one in the 1930s and the other after 1990s — both coincided with periods of deregulation.

Bibliography

Aizenman, Joshua. "Large Hoarding of International Reserves and the Emerging Global Economic Architecture". *Manchester School*, vol. 76, issue 5 (2008): 487–503.

Akyuz, Yilmaz. "Exchange Rate Management, Growth and Stability: National and Regional Policy Options". Mimeographed. 11 March 2009.

Anderson, Jonathan. "Solving China's Rebalancing Puzzle". *Finance and Development*, vol. 44, no. 3 (September 2007).

Andrews, Edmund L. "Greenspan Concedes Error on Regulation". *New York Times*, 23 October 2008.

Ariff, Mohamed. "Time for East Asian to Rethink Its Growth Strategy". *New Straits Times*, 10 September 2009.

Asian Development Bank (ADB). *The U.S. Financial Crisis, Global Financial Turmoil, and Developing Asia: Is the Era of High Growth at an End?* ADB Economics Working Paper Series No. 139, Manila, December 2008.

————. *Asian Development Outlook*. Manila, April 2009.

Asian Regional Integration Center (ARIC). <http://aric.adb.org/aric_database.php>.

Bank of International Settlement (BIS). "Triennial Central Bank Survey of Foreign Exchange and Derivatives Market Activity". <http://www.bis.org/publ/rpfxf07t.htm> (accessed April 2007).

Barbera, Robert J. *The Cost of Capitalism*. New York: McGraw Hill, 2009.

Beja, Edsel L. Jr. "The Myth of Recovery: The Asian Crisis More Than a Decade Later". Quezon City, Philippines: Institute of Philippine Culture, Ateneo de Manila University, 2009.

Berman, Dennis K. "Mood Swing: Deal Boom Wanes as Credit Tightens". *Wall Street Journal Asia*, 7–9 September 2007.

Bernanke, Ben S. "The Global Saving Glut and the U.S. Current Account Deficit". The Homer Jones Lecture, St. Louis, Missouri, 14 April 2005.

———. "Global Imbalances, Recent Developments and Prospects". The Bundesbank Lecture, Berlin, Germany, 11 September 2007.

———. "Asia and the Global Financial Crisis". Speech at the Federal Reserve Bank of San Francisco's Conference on Asia and the Global Financial Crisis, Santa Barbara, California, 19 October 2009.

Bhagwati, Jagdish. "The Capital Myth: The Difference between Trade in Widgets and Dollars". *Foreign Affairs*, vol. 77, no. 3, May/June 1998*a*.

———. "Yes to Free Trade, Maybe to Capital Controls". *The Wall Street Journal*, 16 November 1998*b*, p. A-38.

Blanchard, Olivier. "Current Account Deficits in Rich Countries". Paper presented at the IMF Seventh Jacques Polak Annual Research Conference on Capital Flows. Washington, D.C., 9–10 November 2006.

Blanchard, Olivier, Francesco Giavazzi, and Filipa Sa. "The U.S. Current Account and the Dollar". *Brookings Papers on Economic Activity* 1 (2005): 67–146.

Bowles, Samuel, D.M. Gordon, and T.E. Weisskopf. "Power and Profits: The Social Structure of Accumulation and the Profitability of the Postwar U.S. Economy". *Review of Radical Political Economics*, vol. 18, nos. 1–2 (1986): 132–67.

Bradsher, Keith. "China Slows Purchases of U.S. and Other Bonds". *International Herald Tribune*, 12 April 2009*a*.

———. "China Grows More Picky About Debt". *International Herald Tribune*, 20 May 2009*b*.

Brooks, Rick and Ford Constance Mitchell. "Data Show Bad Loans Permeate Nations, and Pain May Last Years: California's Foreclosure Capital". *The Wall Street Journal*, 12–14 October 2007.

Bruck, Connie. *Predators' Ball: The Inside Story of Drexel Burnham and the Rise of Junk Bond Raiders*. New York: Simon and Schuster, 1988.

Bureau of Economic Analysis. <http://www.bea.gov/interactive.htm>.

Burkett, Paul and Mark Wohar. "Keynes on Investment and the Business Cycle". *Review of Radical Political Economics*, vol. 19, no. 4 (1987): 39–54.

Burkhauser, Richar V., Shuaizhang Feng, Stephen P. Jenkins, and Jeff Larrimore. "Recent Trends in Top Income Share in the USA: Reconciling Estimates from March CPS and IRS Tax Return Data". NBER Working Paper No. 15320, September 2009. <http://papers.nber.org/papers/w15320.pdf>.

Burrough, Bryan and John Helyar. *Barbarians at the Gate: The Fall of RJR Nabisco*. New York: Harper and Row, 1990.

Caballero, Ricardo J., Emmanuel Fahri, and Pierre-Olivier Gourinchas. "An Equilibrium Model of 'Global Imbalances' and Low Interest Rates". *American Economic Review*, vol. 98, no. 1 (2008): 358–93.

Callan, Eoin. "Economists Fear a Wave of Evictions is on the Way". *Financial Times*, 7 September 2007.

Callan, Eoin, Jeremy Grant, and Tony Barber. "No Quick End to Crisis, Says Paulson". *Financial Times*, 12 September 2007.

Capell, Kerry. "Britain's Coming Credit Crisis". *Business Week*, 17 September 2007.

Capra, Fritjoe. *The Turning Point*. London: Flamingo, 1983.

Caprio, Gerard, Daniela Klingebiel, Luc Laeven, and Guillermo Noguera. *Banking Crises Database*. Washington, D.C.: World Bank, October 2003.

Chernow, Ron. *The House of Morgan: An American Banking Dynasty and the Rise of Modern Finance*. New York: Simon and Schuster, 1990.

China Policy Institute (CPI) Report. "China's High Corporate Savings Main Cause of Low Domestic Consumption". School of Contemporary Chinese Studies, University of Nottingham, UK, 16 June 2009.

Chinn, Menzie and Jeffrey Frankel. "Why the Euro will Rival the Dollar". *International Finance*, vol. 11, no. 1 (2008): 49–73.

Cimilluca, Dana and David Enrich. "Banks' Deal — Making Ties Unravel". *The Wall Street Journal Asia*, 19 September 2007.

CNN. "China Backs Alternatives to U.S. Dollar". <http://edition.cnn.com/2009/BUSINESS/03/25/china.currency/> (accessed 16 August 2009).

Cohen, Benjamin J. "Dollar Dominance, Euro Aspirations: Recipe for Discord?" *Journal of Common Market Studies*, vol. 47, no. 4 (September 2009): 741–66.

Commercial Banks Reports (2007). <http//www2/fdic.gov/hsob/index.asp>.

Cookson, Roberts, Sarah O'Connor, and Paul Davies. "Painful Lessons to be Learnt for CDSs". *Financial Times*, 11 January 2008.

Cooper, George. *The Origin of Financial Crises*. New York: Vintage Book, 2008.

Corden, W. Max. "The Asian Crisis: A Perspective After Ten Years". Heinz W. Arndt Memorial Lecture, Canberra, 22 March 2007. <http://econ.unimelb.edu.au/SITE/mcorden/ARNDTLECTURE_compver_july07.pdf> (accessed 10 July 2008).

―――. "China's Exchange Rate Policy, Its Current Account Surplus, and the Global Imbalances". *The Economic Journal*, vol. 119, issue 541 (2009): F430–41.

Corsetti, Giancarlo, Luca Dedola, and Sylvain Leduc. "Productivity, External Balance and Exchange Rates: Evidence on the Transmission Mechanism Among G7 Countries". *NBER International Seminar on Macroeconomics* 2006 (August 2008): 117–78.

Cova, Pietro, Massimiliano Pisani, Nicoletta Batini, and Alessandro Rebucci. "Productivity and Global Imbalances: The Role of Nontradable Total Factor Productivity in Advanced Economies". *IMF Staff Papers* 55 (2008): 312–25.

Credit Suisse. *Emerging Markets Quarterly: Q3 2009*. 17 June 2009.

Crotty, James. "Structural Causes of the Global Financial Crisis: A Critical Assessment of the 'New Financial Architecture'". Working Paper 2008–14. Department of Economics, University of Massachusetts, Amherst. <http://ideas.repec.org/e/pcr99.html>.

Dennis, Brady and Robert O'Harrow Jr. "A Crack in the System". *Washington Post*, 30 December 2008.

Department of Treasury of U.S. Government. *Financial Regulatory Reform — A New Foundation: Rebuilding Financial Supervision and Regulation*. Department of Treasury, U.S. Government, June 2009.

Domhoff, G. William. "Wealth, Income, and Power", September 2005 (updated May 2009). <http://sociology.ucsc.edu/whorulesamerica/power/wealth.html> (accessed 17 July 2009).

————. "Wealth, Income and Power", 2006 <http://sociology.ucsc.edu/whorulesamerica/power.html> (accessed 29 December 2008).

Dooley, Michael P. "A Survey of Literature on Controls over International Capital Transactions". *International Monetary Fund Staff Papers*, vol. 43, no. 4 (December 1996): 639–87.

Dorsch, Gary. "Yen Carry Trade Unwinds". *Global Money Trends*, 16 October 2008.

Dunaway, Steven. *Global Imbalances and the Financial Crisis*. Council on Foreign Relations, Council Special Report No. 44, March 2009.

Duncan, Richard. "Blame the Dollar Standard". *Finance Asia*, September 2007, pp. 35–42.

Economic Report of the President. 1997.

————. 2008.

Economist, The. "Credit Derivatives: At the Risky End of Finance". *The Economist*, vol. 383, no. 8525 (2007*a*): 73–76.

————. "The Trouble with Private Equity". *The Economist*, vol. 384, no. 8536 (2007*b*): 68–70.

————. "The Credit Squeeze". *The Economist*, vol. 384, no. 8540 (2007*c*): 62–64.

————. "America's Central Bank Attempts to Tame a Beast It Once Let Loose". *The Economist*, vol. 384, no. 8545 (2007*d*): 80.

————. "Trade, Exchange Rates. Budget Balances and Interest Rates". *The Economist*, Economic and Financial Indicators, vol. 384, no. 8547 (2007*e*): 98.

————. "A Workers' Manifesto for China". *The Economist*, vol. 385, no. 8550 (2007*f*): 90.

————. "Homeward Bound". *The Economist*, Briefing, vol. 390, no. 8617 (2009*a*): 7–13, 61–62.

————. "Private Equity Return to Earth", 12 February 2009*b*.

————. "The Inefficiency of Markets: Slaves to Some Defunct Economist", 13 June 2009*c*.

————. "Yuan Small Step", 9 July 2009*d* (accessed 16 August 2009*d*. <http://www.economist.com/displayStory.cfm?story_id=13988512>.

Economist's View. "China's Huge Corporate Savings", 4 October 2006. <http://economistsview.typepad.com/economistsview/2006/10/chinas_huge_cor.html>.

Eichengreen, Barry. *Capital Flows and Crises*. Cambridge, MA: The MIT Press, 2003.

Engel, Charles and John H. Rogers. "The U.S. Current Account Deficit and the Expected Share of World Output". *Journal of Monetary Economics* 53 (2006): 1063–93.

Enrich, David. "Citigroup Expects Profit to Tumble in Credit Crisis". *The Wall Street Journal Asia*, 2 October 2007.

Erceg, Christopher J., L. Guerrieri, and C. Gust. "Productivity Growth and the Trade Balance in the 1990s: The Role of Evolving Perceptions". Unpublished. Washington, D.C.: Board of Governors of the Federal Reserve System, 2002.

Farrell, Paul B. "Buffet and Gross Warn: $516 trillion bubble is a disaster waiting to happen". *MarketWatch*, 10 March 2008.

Farzad, Roben. "Let the Blame Begin". *Business Week* 4045 (2007): 32–35.

Farzad, Roben, M. Goldstein, D. Henry, and C. Palmeri. "Not So Smart". *Business Week* 4048 (2007): 30–36.

Federal Deposit Insurance Corporation (FDIC). Historical Statistics on Banking, 2007.

Federal Reserve Board. "Remarks by Chairman Alan Greenspan", April 2002. <http//www.federalreserve.gov/boarddocs/speeches/2002/20020422/default.htm>.

Federal Reserve Board System, Board of Governors. Flow of Funds Z.1 files. <http://www.federalreserve.gov/releases/z1/Current/data.htm>.

Ferguson, Neil. "Global Economy: The Age of Obligation". *Financial Times*, 18 December 2008.

Fogli, Alessandra and Fabrizio Perri. "The 'Great Moderation' and the US External Imbalance". Working Paper No. 12708, November 2006.

Forbes, Kristin. "The Microeconomic Evidence on Capital Controls: No Free Lunch". In *Capital Controls and Capital Flows in Emerging Economies: Policies, Practices and Consequences*, edited by Sebastian Edwards. Chicago: University of Chicago, 2006.

―――. "One Cost of the Chilean Capital Controls: Increased Financial Constraints for Small Traded Firms". *Journal of International Economics*, vol. 71, issue 2 (2007): 294–323.

―――. "Capital Controls". In *The New Palgrave Dictionary of Economics*, 2nd ed., edited by Steven N. Durlauf and Lawrence E. Blume. UK: Palgrave Macmillan, 2008.

Foster, John Bellamy and Fred Magdoff. "Financial Implosion and Stagnation". *Monthly Review*, December 2008. <http//www.monthlyreview.org/081201foster-magdoff.php>.

Freeland, Chrystin. "Lunch with the FT: Larry Summer". *Financial Times*, 10 July 2009.

Galbraith, James K. *The Predator State*. New York: Free Press, 2008.

Galbraith, John K. *A Short History of Financial Euphoria*. New York: Penguin, 1993.

―――. *The Great Crash 1929*. Boston: Houghton Mifflin, 1997.

Gapper, John. "This Greed Was Beyond Irresponsible". *Financial Times*, 17 September 2008.

Gilani, Shah. "The Real Reason for the Global Financial Crisis", 2008*a*. <http://www/moneymorning.com/2008/09/18/credit-default-swaps>.

―――. "The Credit Crisis and the Real Story Behind the Collapse of AIG", 2008*b*. <http://www.moneymorning.com/2008/09/22/credit-default-swaps-2>.

————. "Federal Government Grants AIG a New Bailout Package", 2008*c*. <http://www.contrarianprofits.com/articles/federal-government-grants-aig-a-new-bailout-package/8249>.

Gilbert, Mark. "Bernanke Bonus Mustn't Make Hedge-Fund Guys Blush". *The Star*, 28 August 2009.

Giles, Chris. "Bank of England Sees Stoicism Come under Fire". *Financial Times*, 7 September 2007*a*.

————. "Credit Crunch-Central Banks Intervene: Coordinated Action Attracts Praise". *Financial Times,* 13 December 2007*b*.

Glick, Reuven and Kenneth Rogoff. "Global Versus Country-Specific Productivity Shocks and the Current Account". *Journal of Monetary Economics* 35 (1995): 159–92.

Goodman, Peter S. "Taking Hard New Look at a Greenspan Legacy". *International Herald Tribune*, 8 October 2008.

Greenspan, Alan. "Risk Transfer and Financial Stability", 5 May 2005. <http://www.federalreserve.gov/boarddocs/speeches/2005/20050505/default.htm> (accessed 10 August 2009).

Guha, Krishna. "A Global Vision". *Financial Times*, 17 September 2007.

————. "US Aims for Safety Allied to Dynamism". *Financial Times*, 18 June 2009.

Harvey, David. *A Brief History of Neoliberalism.* New York: Oxford University Press, 2007.

Henriques, Diana B. "U.S. Bailout Monitor Sees Lack of A Coherent Plan". *New York Times*, 2 December 2008.

Hodges, Michael W. *Grandfather Economic Series*, March 2007. <http://mwhodges.home.att.net/nat-debt/debt-nat.htm>.

Hunt, Ben and Alessandro Rebucci. "The US Dollar and the Trade Deficit: What Accounts for the Late 1990s?" *International Finance* 8 (2005): 399–434.

International Financial Statistics of the International Monetary Fund (hereafter cited as IFS).

International Herald Tribune. 3 September 2007.

————. 20 September 2007.

International Monetary Fund (hereafter cited as IMF). "The Quiet Integrationist". *Finance and Development*, vol. 43, no. 1, March

2006*a*. <http://www.imf.org/external/pubs/ft/fandd/2006/03/people.htm>.

———. "Oil Prices and Global Imblances". World Economic Outlook, April 2006*b*. <http://www.imf.org/external/pubs/ft/weo/2006/01/index.htm>.

———. "Exchange Rates and the Adjustment of External Imbalances". *World Economic Outlook*, April 2007.

———. "Asia and Pacific Global Crisis: The Asian Context". *Regional Economic Outlook*, May 2009*a*.

———. "Contractionary Forces Receding But Weak Recovery Ahead". *World Economic Outlook Update*, 8 July 2009*b*.

———. *Sustaining the Recovery. World Economic Outlook*, October 2009*c*.

Johnston, David Cay. "Richest are Leaving Even the Rich Far Behind". *New York Times*, 5 June 2005. <www.nytimes.com>.

———. "Average Pay in Investment Banking is Ten Times that Elsewhere". *International Herald Tribune*, 3 September 2007.

Kahneman, Daniel, Paul Slovic, and Amos Tversky. *Judgment Under Uncertainty: Heuristics and Biases*. New York: Cambridge University Press, 1982,

Keynes, John Maynard. *The General Theory of Employment, Interest, and Money*. New York: Harvest/HBJ Book, 1964.

Khor, Hoe Ee and Kit Wei Zheng. "Ten Years from the Financial Crisis: Managing the Challenges Posed by Capital Flows". In *Lessons from the Asian Financial Crisis*, edited by Richard Carney. New York: Routledge, 2008.

Kindleberger, Charles P. *Manias, Panics, and Crashes: A History of Financial Crisis*. New York: John Wiley & Sons Inc., 2000.

Koo, Richard C. *The Holy Grail of Macro Economics*. Singapore: Wiley & Sons (Asia), 2008.

Kregel, Jan A. "A New Triffin Paradox for the Global Economy". Remarks prepared for The Federal Council of Economists and the Regional Council of Economists of Rio de Janeiro meeting of the 13th Brazilian Congress of Economists and the 7th Congress of the Association of Economists from Latin-American and the Caribbean, 15 September 1999. <http://iml.umkc.edu/econ/economics/faculty/Kregel/Readings/Triffin.pdf>.

Krugman, Paul. *The Return of Depression Economics and the Crisis of 2008*. New York: W.W. Norton and Company, 2009*a*.

————. "Making Banking Boring". *International Herald Tribune*, 9 April 2009*b*.

————. *Lionel Robbins Memorial Lectures*. London: London School of Economics, June 2009*c*.

Kwok, V.W. "Collapse of Carry Trade Could Choke New Zealand". Forbes.com, 3 June 2007.

Kydland, Finn E. and Edward C. Prescott. "Time to Build and Aggregate Fluctuations". *Econometrica*, vol. 50, no. 6 (1982): 1345–70.

Langley, Monica, Deborah Solomon, and Matthew Karnitschnig. "A Wave Engulfing Wall Street Swamps the World's Largest Insurer". *Wall Street Journal Asia*, 19–21 September 2008.

Larsen, Peter Thal and Ivar Simensen. "Ackermann Urges Banks to Reveal Losses from Credit Crunch". *Financial Times*, 6 September 2007.

Lee, J.W. and W.J. McKibbin. "Domestic Investment and External Imbalances in East Asia". CAMA Working Paper 4. Canberra: Centre for Applied Macroeconomic Analysis, ANU College of Business and Economics, 2007.

Leonhardt, David. "Soft Landing Unlikely for the Housing Slump". *International Herald Tribune*, 20 September 2007.

Lewis, Michael. *Liar's Poker*. New York: Penguin, 1990.

Lim, Michael Mah-Hui. "Old Wine in New Bottle: Subprime Mortgage Crisis — Causes and Consequences". The Levy Economics Institute of Bard College, Working Paper No. 532, April 2008.

Litvinsky, Marina. "How Wall Street Paid for its Own Funeral". *Third World Resurgence*, no. 223 (March 2009): 2–3.

Long, John B. Jr. and Charles Plosser. "Real Business Cycles". *Journal of Political Economy*, vol. 91, no. 1 (1983): 39–69.

Lucas, Robert E. Jr. "Understanding Business Cycles". *Carnegie-Rochester Conference Series on Public Policy* 5 (1977): 7–29.

Maddison, Angus. *Chinese Economic Performance in the Long Run.* 2nd ed. Revised and Updated 960–2030 AD. Development Centre Studies, OECD, 2007.

Magud, Nicolas and Carmen M. Reinhart. "Capital Controls: An Evaluation". NBER Working Papers 11973. Cambridge, MA: National Bureau of Economic Research, 2006.

Martinez, Elizabeth and Arnoldo Garcia. "What is 'Neo-liberalism': A Brief Definition". *CorpWatch*, 22 March 2001. <http://www.hartford-hwp.com/archives/25/111.html> (accessed 25 August 2009).

Martinez, Mark A. *The Myth of the Free Market: The Role of the State in a Capitalist Economy.* Sterling, Virgina: Kumarian Press, 2009.

Masaki, Hisane. "Asian Monetary Fund?", 10 May 2007. <http://english.ohmynews.com/articleview/article_view.asp?at_code=409447> (accessed 16 August 2009).

Mendoza, Enrique G., Vincenzo Quadrini, and J. Rios-Rull. "Financial Integration, Financial Development, and Global Imbalances". *Journal of Political Economy*, vol. 117, no. 3 (2009): 371–416.

Miller, Rich and Allison Sider. "Surging U.S. Savings Rate Reduces Dependence on China (Update2)". Bloomberg.com, 26 June 2009. <http://www.bloomberg.com/apps/news?pid=20601103&sid=aMl2N_xsMPT4>.

Minsky, Hyman P. "Central Banking and Money Market Changes". *Quarterly Journal of Economics*, vol. 71, no. 2 (1957): 171–87.

———. *Stabilizing An Unstable Economy.* New Haven: Yale University Press, 1986.

Moffitt, Michael. *The World's Money: International Banking from Bretton Woods to the Brink of Insolvency.* New York: Simon and Schuster, 1983.

Monetary Authority of Singapore (hereafter cited as MAS). *Financial Stability Review.* Singapore: MAS, November 2008.

New York Times. "IMF Predicts $1.4 Trillion in Losses from Crisis", 7 October 2008. <http://www.nytimes.com/2008/10/07/business/worldbusiness/07iht-07imf.16753576.html> (accessed 10 October 2009).

Ng, Serena. "Tenuous Return for Debt". *Wall Street Journal Asia*, 13 September 2007.

Norris, Floyd. "U.S. Securities Lose Their Charm for Investors Overseas". *International Herald Tribune*, February 2009.

Obstfeld, Maurice and Kenneth Rogoff. "The Unsustainable US Current Account Position Revisited". In *G7 Current Account Imbalances: Sustainability and Adjustment*, edited by Richard Clarida. Chicago: University of Chicago Press, 2007.

Ocampo, Jose Antonio. "Special Drawing Rights and the Reform of the Global Reserve System". Intergovernmental Group of Twenty-Four, 2009. <http://www.g24.org/jao0909.pdf>.

Palley, Thomas I. "Financialization: What It Is and Why It Matters". Working Paper No. 525. New York: The Levy Economics Institute of Bard College, 2007.

Papadimitriou, Dimitri, Edward Chilcote, and Gennaro Zezza. "Are Housing Prices, Household Debt, and Growth Sustainable?" *Strategic Analysis.* Annandale-on-Hudson, NY: The Levy Economics Institute of Bard College, January 2006.

People's Daily Online. "Obama's regulatory reform in right direction, but not enough, says Stiglitz", 26 June 2009. <http://english. peopledaily.com.cn/90001/90778/90858/90864/6687160.html> (accessed 31 August 2009).

Perelstein, Julia S. "Macroeconomic Imbalances in the United States and Their Impact on the International Financial System". Working Paper No. 554. New York: The Levy Economics Institute of Bard College, January 2009.

Persaud, Avinash. "When Currency Empires Fall". Gresham Lectures, Gresham College, United Kingdom, 7 October 2004. <http://www. gresham.ac.uk/event.asp?EventId=260&PageId=108>.

Philippon, Thomas and Ariell Reshef. "Wages and Human Capital in the U.S. Financial Industry, 1900–2006". National Bureau of Economic Research, Working Paper No. 14644, January 2009.

Phillips, Kevin. *Bad Money*. New York: Penguin Group, 2008.

Pio, Hak-Kil. "Global Financial Crisis and the Korean Economy: Issues and Perspectives". In *Korea's Economy 2009*, vol. 25.

A publication of Korea Economic Institute and Korea Institute for International Economic Policy, 2009.

Plender, John. "Originative Sin: The future of Banking". *Financial Times*, 4 January 2009.

Politi, James. "Banks to Sell First Data Loan at Discount". *Financial Times*, 14 September 2007.

Posner, Richard A. *A Failure of Capitalism: The Crisis of '08 and the Descent into Depression*. Cambridge: Harvard University Press, 2009*a*.

———. "A Failure of Capitalism — Financial Regulatory Reform: I". *The Atlantic*, 22 June 2009*b*. <http://correspondents.theatlantic.com/richard_posner/2009/06/financial_regulatory_reform_i.php> (accessed 24 August 2009*b*).

Prasad, Eswar M., Kenneth Rogoff, S.J. Wei, and M.A. Kose. "Effects of Financial Globalization on Developing Countries: Some Empirical Evidence". International Monetary Fund Occasional Paper No. 220 (2003): 1–86.

Raja, Kanaga. "Financial Deregulation at Root of Current Global Crisis". *Third World Network*, 26 March 2009. <http://www.twnside.org.sg/title2/finance/2009/twninfofinance20090305.htm>.

Rajan, Raghuram. "Perspectives on Global Imbalances". Remarks at the Global Financial Imbalances Conference, London, United Kingdom, 23 January 2006.

———. "Firms in Emerging Markets to Gain from Demand Shift". *The Star*, 12 August 2009.

Reich, Robert B. *Supercapitalism*. New York: Alfred A. Knopf, 2007.

Reilly, David and Carrick Mollenkamp. "Hazards are Lurking in 'Conduits', Adding to Subprime Concern". *Wall Street Journal Asia*, 31 August–2 September 2007.

Reinhart, Carmen M. and Kenneth S. Roghoff. "Is the 2007 U.S. Sub-prime Financial Crisis So Different? An International Historical Comparison". <http://www.economics.harvard.edu/files/faculty/51_Is_The_US_Subprime_Crisis_So_Different.pdf> (accessed 10 March 2008).

————. "The Aftermath of Financial Crises". <http://www.economics. harvard.edu/files/faculty/51_Aftermath.pdf> (accessed 11 August 2009).

Roach, David. "Update: New Monetarism — The Music Stops". *Independent Strategy*, 27 July 2007.

Roach, Stephen. "What Global Saving Glut?" Morgan Stanley, Global Economic Forum, 5 July 2005.

————. *The Next Asia: Opportunities and Challenges for a New Globalization*. Hoboken, N.J.: John Wiley & Sons, 2009.

Rodrik, Dani. "Who Needs Capital Account Convertibility?" *Essays in International Finance*, No. 207 (May 1998): 55–65.

Roubini, Nouriel and Brad Setser. "The U.S. as a Net Debtor: The Sustainability of the U.S. External Imbalances". Unpublished manuscript. Stern School of Business, New York University, 2004.

Saez, Emmauel. "Striking it Richer: The Evolution of Top Incomes in the United States". Mimeographed. Department of Economics, University of California, Berkeley, 2008.

Saft, James. "Sharp Drop in Services Bodes Ill". *International Herald Tribune*, 8 February 2008.

Samuelson, Robert. "Capitalism's Enemies Within". *Washington Post*, 23 January 2008.

Saporito, Bill. "How AIG Became Too Big to Fail". *Time*, 30 March 2009.

Scheuble, K. "U.S. Fed's Target Federal Funds Interest Rate History (Table)". *Bloomberg News*, 29 April 2009.

Schwartz, Nelson D. "The Fallout from Foreclosures begins to Engulf Middle-Class Communities". *International Herald Tribune*, 2 September 2007.

Sender, Henny. "Credit Insurance Hampers Restructuring Plan". *Financial Times*, 12 May 2009*a*.

————. "Greenlight Capital Founder Calls for CDS Ban". *Financial Times*, 6 November 2009*b*.

Shiller, Robert J. *Irrational Exuberance*. New Jersey: Princeton University Press, 2000.

————. "A Failure to Control the Animal Spirits". *Financial Times*, 9 March 2009*a*.

————. "Why Home Prices May Keep Falling". *Financial Times*, 6 June 2009*b*.

Singer, Jason, Carrick Mollenkamp, and Simon Kennedy. "UBS Takes Subprime Hit: $3.44 Billion Write-Down". Money and Investing, *Wall Street Journal Asia*, 2 October 2007.

Skeel Jr., D.A. and Frank Partnoy. "The Promise and Perils of Credit Derivatives". San Diego Legal Studies Paper No. 07–74 (2007).

Sorkin, Andrew R. and Mary W. Walsh. "AIG May Get Billions More in Bailout". *International Herald Tribune*, 10 November 2008.

Soros, George. *The* Alchemy *of Finance*. New York: John Wiley, 2003.

Standard & Poor's. "Case-Schiller Home Price". <http://www2. standardandpoors.com/portal/site/sp/en/us/page.topic/indices_ csmahp> (accessed 8 July 2009).

Stiglitz, Joseph. "Boats, Planes and Capital Flows". *Financial Times*, 25 March 1998.

Straits Times. "Why Citi Had to be Rescued", 25 November 2008.

Summers, Lawrence H. "Some Skeptical Observations on Real Business Cycle Theory". *Federal Reserve Bank of Minneapolis Quarterly Review* 10 (Fall 1986): 23–27.

SustainableMiddleClass.com. <http://blog.sustainablemiddleclass. com/?page_id=162>.

Taibbi, Matt. "The Big Takeover". *Rolling Stone*, 19 March 2009. <http://www.rollingstone.com/politics/story/26793903/the_big_ takeover>.

Tanzi, Alex. "U.S. December Home Delinquency, Foreclosure Rates (Table for YTD ending December 2008)". *Bloomberg News*, 15 January 2009 (accessed 23 June 2009).

Taub, Stephen. "The Top 25 Moneymakers: The New Tycoons". *Alpha Magazine*, 20 April 2007. <http://www.alphamagazine. com/Article.aspx?ArticleID=1328498&PositionID=25424>.

Taylor, Andrew. "More Private Equity Disclosure Urged". *Financial Times*, 12 September 2007.

Taylor, Edward. "Deutsche Bank Sets Charges, Joining Rivals". *Wall Street Journal Asia*, 4 October 2007.

Thaler, Richard and Werner W. de Bondt. "Does the Stock Market Overreact?" *Journal of Finance*, vol. 40, issue 3 (1985): 793–805.

Tobin, James. "A Proposal for International Monetary Reform". *Eastern Economic Journal*, vol. 4, issues 3–4 (1978): 153–59.

Triffin, Robert. *Gold and the Dollar Crisis*. Revised edition. New Haven: Yale University Press, 1961.

———. *Our International Monetary System: Yesterday, Today and Tomorrow*. New York: Random House, 1968.

Ubiq Consultancy/LLC, n.d. "Why Did Emerging Markets Remove Capital Controls in Recent Years?" <http://www.ubiqconsultancy. com/docs/capital_controls.pdf> (accessed 13 August 2009).

UNCTAD. *The Global Economic Crisis: Systemic Failures and Multilateral Remedies*. Report by the UNCTAD Secretariat Task Force on Systemic Issues and Economic Cooperation, 2009.

United Nations. *Report of the Commission of Experts of the President of United Nations General Assembly on Reforms of the International Monetary and Financial System*. Prepared for the Conference on the World and Financial and Economic Crisis and its Impact on Development, New York, 24–26 June 2009.

Washington, Jeremy G. "Crisis Highlights Need for Fresh Financial Regulation". *Financial Times*, 6 September 2007.

Wehrfritz, George. "Then They All Fall Down". *Newsweek International* CL (10) (2007): 36–38.

Whalen, Charles J. "Hyman Minsky's Theory of Capitalist Development". The Jerome Levy Economics Institute of Bard College, Working Paper No. 277, August 1999. <http://papers.ssrn.com/ sol3/papers.cfm?abstract_id=180070>.

———. "A Minsky Perspective on the Global Recession of 2009". Utica College, Cornell University School of Industrial and Labor Relations, Research on Money and Finance, Discussion Paper No. 12, 1 July 2009. <http://www.soas.ac.uk/rmf/papers/ file52179.pdf>.

Wikinvest. "Mortgage Equity Withdrawal (MEW)". <http://www.wikinvest.com/wiki/Mortgage_Equity_Withdrawal_(MEW)> (accessed 10 December 2008).

Wikipedia. "Household income in the United States". <http://en.wikipedia.org/wiki/Household_income_in_the_United_States> (accessed 10 January 2009*a*).

―――. "United States public debt". <http://en.wikipedia.org/wiki/United_States_public_debt> (accessed 15 August 2009*b*).

―――. "List of countries by foreign exchange reserves". <http://en.wikipedia.org/wiki/List_of_countries_by_foreign_exchange_reserves#List_of_states_by_foreign_exchange_reserves> (accessed 15 August 2009*c*).

Wolf, Martin. "Unfettered Finance is Fast Reshaping the Global Economy". *Financial Times*, 18 June 2007*a*.

―――. "The Policy Challenge of Rescuing the World Economy". *Financial Times*, 12 September 2007*b*.

―――. "Why Regulators Should Intervene in Bankers' Pay". *Financial Times*, 16 January 2008.

World Bank. *World Development Indicators 2007*. Washington, D.C.: World Bank, 2007.

―――. *Battling the Forces of Global Recession*. East Asia and Pacific Update. Washington, D.C., April 2009.

Yap, Rodney and Dave Pierson. "Subprime Mortgage Related Losses Exceed $1.6 Trillion". *Bloomberg News*, 13 August 2009.

Yoshitomi, Masaru. "Global Imbalances and East Asian Monetary Cooperation". In *Toward an East Asian Exchange Rate Regime*, edited by Duck-Koo Chung and Barry Eichengreen. Washington, D.C.: Brookings Institution, 2007.

Index

About the Authors

Michael Lim Mah-Hui is a Senior Fellow at the Asian Public Intellectuals' Program, Nippon Foundation. He is also a Senior Fellow at the Socio-Economic and Environmental Research Institute (SERI) in Penang, Malaysia.

Dr Lim's professional background spans thirty years as an international banker and academician. He has worked in major international banks, including Chemical Bank (now JP Morgan Chase) in New York and Tokyo, Credit Suisse First Boston in Singapore and Hong Kong, Deutsche Bank in Singapore and Jakarta, Standard Chartered Bank in Jakarta, and the Asian Development Bank in Manila. Prior to his banking career, he did research in and taught Political Economics and Sociology at Duke University, Temple University and the University of Malaya.

Dr Lim has a multi-disciplinary background in finance, economics and politics. He received his B.A. (Honours) in Economics from the University of Malaya; a Masters in International Affairs, a Masters in Sociology, and a Ph.D. in Development Studies from the University of Pittsburgh; and Certificate of Business Administration from Wharton School, University of Pennsylvania.

Most recently, he has extensively researched and delivered public lectures on the global financial crisis throughout Asia.

Lim Chin is a Professor of Economics at the Department of Strategy and Policy, NUS Business School, National University of Singapore (NUS). Prior to joining NUS in 1986, he taught at the University of Western Ontario, Canada. His publications on the behaviour of firms, market structure, market contestability, labour contract structure, public goods and urban economics appear in leading academic journals such as *American Economic Review, Journal of Economic Theory, Rand Journal of Economics, Economica, European Economic Review, Canadian Journal of Economics, Journal of Public Economic Theory, Economics Letters,* and *Transportations Research.* Based on the frequency of citations of his publications in the Social Science Citation Index, he is listed in Mark Blaug's (2nd and 3rd editions), "Who's Who in Economics". He has consulted widely for both private and public organizations. At the height of the financial panic in 2008–09, he wrote several articles on the crisis, and edited a book *Globalisation and Financial Crisis.*